This is the candid autobiography of one young person's search to find himself and the deeper meaning of his life. Amidst his search, he stumbles onto a stinging truth: his life plan is unreal, for he has made an idol of all the virtues and values his evangelical faith and suburban lifestyle tattooed on his soul. In the end he returns home to where his journey began, albeit with a scarred bravado and a faith barnacled but more transparent and believable."

BILL ENRIGHT
Director, Lake Family Institute
on Faith & Giving

This gem of a story held me from first page to last. Pete Gall can write!

NATE LARKIN
author of *Samson and the Pirate Monks:*
Calling Men to Authentic Brotherhood

A truly humble account of a man's journey through Christian America. Pete's struggles and insight hit home with me as it did others I know who read this book.

JOHN DALE
Staff Sergeant in the Army National Guard
and a combat veteran

Have you ever turned on lights in a basement only to see a flurry of critters running for cover? With a wry mix of insight and transparency, Pete Gall lights up a reader's soul. Thank God for a book that becomes an honest friend! But Pete does more than expose our brokenness. He tugs us to join him in walking, stumbling, running — whatever our state and status — into the arms of a God who loves us. This book is for everyone, absolutely everyone, who knows what a prodigal is and needs!

R. N. (RON) FROST
staff, Barnabas International

———

Pete Gall runs a gauntlet of self-absorption, religious dysfunction, and disgust at the tawdry meanness of his own spiritual veneer — the archetypal path of contemporary evangelicalism. With humor and honesty as his only protections, he takes a beating (and the candid reader will too), but keeps his feet moving out of a genuine hunger for God.

GREG PAUL
author of *God in the Alley*
and *The Twenty Piece Shuffle*

———

I knew Pete could communicate — just not so honestly or about himself. I laughed, I cried, and all the while I am grateful for funny prophetic voices that challenge my own story and shine the light of God's love right where the darkness is most dense — the human heart.

BILL KNOTT
World Vision

MY BEAUTIFUL IDOL

PETE GALL

ZONDERVAN®

ZONDERVAN.com/
AUTHORTRACKER
follow your favorite authors

▌ZONDERVAN®

My Beautiful Idol
Copyright © 2008 by Peter D. Gall

Requests for information should be addressed to:
Zondervan, *Grand Rapids, Michigan 49530*

Library of Congress Cataloging-in-Publication Data

Gall, Pete
    My beautiful idol / Pete Gall.
      p. cm.
    ISBN 978-0-310-28310-2 (softcover)
    1. Gall, Pete, 1971- 2. Christian biography—United States. I. Title.
    BR1725.G35A3 2008
    277.3'083092—dc22
    [B]   2007047705

Internet addresses (websites, blogs, etc.) and telephone numbers printed in this book are offered as a resource to you. These are not intended in any way to be or imply an endorsement on the part of Zondervan, nor do we vouch for the content of these sites and numbers for the life of this book.

In order to protect the privacy of individuals in this story, some names have been changed.

Interior design by Beth Shagene

Printed in the United States of America

08 09 10 11 12 13 14 • 23 22 21 20 19 18 17 16 15 14 13 12 11 10 9 8 7 6 5 4 3 2 1

For my family,
by whom I am well loved.

CONTENTS

I suddenly became very afraid that I had been doing all the right things without truly "seeing" anyone. Who had experienced invisibility because of my own blindness?

As I relived my time in Denver while writing this book, one thing set itself deep within me: Real life, a life of love, is so, so much more and so much better than we've been taught.

My intention was to write the book I wish I could have encountered during my time in Denver. And back to my wife's insight, I think in some cases it's good to be a butt. I don't think I tend to listen to anyone who isn't one. I've always needed a little saltiness — saltiness I can work with. Sweet I can get on Christian TV, and if I want a little folksy pabulum, I can go to church.

"Like that, right there," Christine will say about my buttishness.

Whatever.

One last thing that I'd like to say to you, and I hope it will make it through the editorial process. I truly, deeply care how this book impacts you, and I offer it to you in love as an act of worship to the God who suffers me and makes me squint and grin at the world he's made.

Writing this book was important for me as I sought to make better sense of who I am and what it means to have meaningful faith ... the sort that can flex and grow and be beautiful without needing me to shine it up and pose it just so. If spending the time with my heart and my mind in your hands gives you reason to thank God for the life you've been given, know that I've prayed that for you, and I would love to hear your story.

PETE GALL
Indianapolis, IN
October 2007

Part I

The Wisdom of Cynics

CHAPTER 1

LIES FOR THE SAKE OF LIES

I'm the fat blond guy on the corner in the African print shirt, squeezing himself into the yellow taxi.

"Burritoville on Addison near Wrigley," I direct.

It's 7:15, Wednesday night, August 3, 1994. I work late most nights because my ad agency buys cab rides and dinners for people who work past 7:00. Once a month my boss complains that as a man I'm taking politically incorrect advantage of a loophole in a politically correct policy intended to protect the safety of female employees. He says that I should be taking the bus and buying my own dinner. Maybe, but all I care about is that I get four giant chorizo burritos and four Mountain Dews a week for free, and I don't have to deal with the bus. And we both know that even my overtime, including dinners and cab rides, is cheaper than what any of the experienced employees would cost him.

"Long day at work?" the driver asks in a Russian accent.

"Yeah," I reply, sizing the man up. Lately I've been exploring the power and joy of lying to strangers. "I write for an advertising agency."

This part is true. The world's largest agency, in fact. And a fact of which I am quite proud. It wasn't easy getting into the industry, but somehow last year, with plenty of ego-stroking, I landed a great job with big-name clients.

"Anything I see?"

"Ever read your shampoo bottle?" I ask. "The directions on the back?"

"Yeah."

"I revolutionized the hair care industry with one word." This is the lie.

"How?"

"I added the word 'repeat' to the end of the directions. My client increased profits by 150 percent in a year." I make the number up at random.

"Interesting," he says, but he's clearly not all that impressed, and we return to silence as he weaves heart-stoppingly through traffic for a few blocks. Then he says, "Even if every person washed their hair twice, that would only be double. Why did profits go up even more?"

"Good insight," I say, practicing my client skill of congratulating people's intelligence when they show even the slightest mental effort. "At first our goal was just to increase sales — you know, get people to use more. And it worked. People quickly learned that they were supposed to shampoo twice. Then the shampoo makers realized that using twice as much shampoo was actually very hard on people's hair. So they diluted the stuff, which made it a lot less expensive to produce." I lean forward, locking his eyes in the rearview mirror to force him to listen, just to see how the trick will work. "And that's when things really took off. People who were only shampoo-ing once needed conditioner because the shampoo wasn't working on its own, and people who were following the directions needed conditioner because the shampoo was frying their hair. All told, my client improved its profits by 150 percent, and the rest of the industry followed suit." I sit back in my seat. "Of course, that was just the first year — I've been working on other projects since then."

"This is what you do, write tricky words?"

"That's my job. We call it 'creating a need.' I write the songs that make the young girls sing. I write the songs of love and hair and shiny things," I sing. "I write the songs, I write the songs." *It's Mr. Manilow to you.* Most nights it takes a couple of hours and at least a couple of beers to slow the free association required to keep up the "talented young copywriter" role I play at work. And being so young, I feel like I have to be the one who makes the joke first, or who has the comeback ready, because the worst thing is to be seen as too young and too green — or gullible. It's exhausting to be driven by the sort of fear that tells me to "fake it 'til you make it"; but it was too hard to land this job to crash and burn now that I have it.

"What others?" he asks.

"You mean what other needs do I create?"

"Yeah."

"All of them, my friend," I say, practicing the trick of famil-iarity with a stranger to build power. "Needs are all made up, and there will always be new ones. Things you don't even know about today are things that I'll make sure you won't be able to live without tomorrow."

He scowls a little at the cliché and the dark truth behind it.

"Don't think of it as a bad thing, or at least don't think of me as the bad guy. It's the nature of man. We're all after something to tell us about ourselves. We all want to be on the right teams. And we don't care much where the things that identify us — in the sense that they give us our identity — come from. In fact, the easier they come, the better. Take Coke versus Pepsi, for example. Do I see myself as more of a loyal traditionalist with family values? If so, I buy Coke to remind myself about it. Or do I see myself as more of a hip fun member of the next generation, in which case Pepsi is my drink of choice? Exactly the same thing with McDonald's and Burger King, Ford and Honda, IBM and Apple. We build a whole world around that sort of stuff. We measure who we are and tell other people who we are by labels we slap on our lives. It's not new, either – it's how we've picked our religions for generations."

"Hmm." He doesn't care, but I think it's fascinating. Plus, if I speak with enough confidence he'll let me feel like maybe I'm right.

I do think I'm right, though. I'm not happy about the truth, but at least there's an ego stroke in feeling like I'm one of the rare people who's willing to face it. Once I saw it, I started seeing it everywhere. For example, the other day I picked up a gem from a program about the collector crab. Of the genus *schizophroida*, which is Greek for *bearer of split likeness*. The collector crab, or decorator crab, as it's also called, attaches to his shell bits of what it finds on the sea floor. According to the narrator with the British accent, the idea is to protect itself by becoming invisible to its natural enemy, the squid. Makes sense, I thought. People do the same thing. And like the collector crab, which sometimes chooses camouflage that actually makes the crab easier to spot, we can't ever be all that sure about the stuff we pick up and attach to our shells; all we can do is grab what looks good to us. That's where I come in. My job in advertising is to sell people, all bearers of the likeness of God, baubles to attach to their personal shells. Labels we slap on our lives, like products, services, impressions, approaches, tones, movements, whatever — anything that can help build a consumer's "personal brand." Our god is our personal brand, our existential self, our chosen reflection or explanation or defense or excuse to the world. It's how we hide from the "squids" in our lives, which show up in the form of evil or fear or shame or a host of other things we work furiously to avoid.

And the squids are everywhere, looking to devour us. We're desperate to do what we can to camouflage ourselves — from fig leaves to 401(k)s, we're all about covering our nakedness. We scurry along through the dark corners of our worlds looking for hiding places we can take with us. And so long as we remain uneaten, it feels like it's working.

My job is to help my clients sell camouflage to frightened crabs. What's tough is that I'm a crab too. It's why I bluster in front of strangers, or tell lies for the sake of telling lies and getting away with it. Still, something inside of me resents this taxi driver for letting me get away with my sinister bravado. I don't want to be right about the world. I want him to disprove my cynicism, not just endure me. I want him to argue against me, to try to see me, to let me know if my camouflage is really working. Or better yet, I want him to show me a way to live that doesn't require the camouflage. The truth is that I'm so desperate to be myself — but still adequate and loved — that I'm willing to look for clues anywhere. Even from cab drivers. But he doesn't care. He has his own hiding places to worry about — and there's no way he'll risk his security by admitting I'm messing with it. Admitting you're hiding is too much like admitting you're vulnerable, and, like most people, he chooses not to talk about such things.

We drive the rest of the way to Burritoville in silence. I casually over-tip him, and ask for a receipt for my expense report.

CHAPTER 2

Happy Birthday, Sweetheart

I walk the three blocks from Burritoville toward Lake Shore, carrying my dinner in a brown paper bag. As I enter the courtyard of my apartment building, I see Betsy outside my door waiting for me. I turn and duck back around the corner of the building before she notices me. I sit with my back against the wall and unwrap the burrito. She can wait.

Twenty-four hours earlier we were out for my birthday dinner. Hancock building, 95th floor. Window table facing north. I wore a tie. She wore a low-cut, black spaghetti strap dress over her perfect body, pearls resting proudly on her delicate collarbones, double French braids in her chestnut hair. She owned me. My birthday was also our four-and-a-half-year anniversary. I'd been shopping for engagement rings for weeks, but before we'd even ordered dinner she dropped the bomb.

"You said there was nothing there, Betsy."

"I was lying."

"How long?"

"Six months."

"So the roses did mean something."

"That was at the very beginning."

"And last Thursday?"

"I've been with him."

"What?"

"Every Thursday. I've been with him every Thursday."

"Does he know about me?"

"He thinks we broke up."

"Why didn't we?"

"I love you."

I was staring at her with my stunned mouth half-open when the waiter breezed up and asked for our orders.

"I'll take the lobster and another Glenfiddich," I said.

As she ordered, I looked out the window toward my apartment. My stinking Chicago apartment, in stinking Chicago. I hated Chicago. I hated Chicago people. I hated Chicago sports teams and sports fans. I hated the Chicago accent and the stupidity it highlighted in the people who had it. I hated Betsy's ancient insane parents, and her brothers and their beer and muscle cars and posture of protecting her against me. Like *she* was the one who needed protecting. I hated life in Chicago.

But I thought this was going to be it. I thought Betsy's family, with all of their arguing and drinking and bigotry, was going to be my family. I thought I was going to be in Chicago forever because that's the only place Betsy could see herself. All at once it was unraveling.

Outside the dining room window, a thousand feet up in the night air, I suddenly noticed a spider clinging to a strand of web, a filament of hope spun from itself. Were there even bugs up this high for spiders to catch? How in the world did it get so far from the ground? How long would that take, to climb all the way from terra firma? Four-and-a-half years, maybe? Did it have any idea how far it was from the ground? Did it have any fear, dangling a foot from the glass? I have never experienced a moment I wanted to escape so badly, and it's the only time I've ever wanted to trade places with a spider, if only the spider could have been convinced that it wasn't getting the short end of the deal.

What would my family say about the end of the relationship? Of course, my mother would assume I did something to ruin it. What would I even tell them? My friends were easy; they'd been sick of Betsy for years and would immediately take me out drinking to celebrate. My coworkers, Brett and Tony in particular, would moan like I'd missed the game-winning field goal. They found it absurd that Betsy and I had never slept together, and were determined to find the right scenario for it to happen. I told them we hadn't because I knew it wouldn't be worth dealing with her shame if we did.

"I do, really."

"Love me?" I asked, raising my eyebrows sarcastically.

"Yes."

"You've always said he was such a jerk."

"He is."

"So . . ."

"So that's what makes it all so hard. So confusing."

"You're confused because you're cheating on me with a jerk?"

"Yeah."

"Have you slept with him?"

"That's none of your business."

"What?" I did one of those coughing/laughing things on the *wh*.

"I'm not going to talk to you about our sex life."

"'Our' sex life. Are you serious?" I stopped and took a sip of my Scotch because I could see that she was about to cry, and the last thing I had the patience for was crying from her right then. After a long pause and the preparation of a dinner roll, I tried again.

"I won't make you say it, Betsy. Can I ask you this, though? Do you and I have a sex life?"

There was a candle on the table, and her skin looked so perfect in the dim yellow light. Her eyes were wet and red when she looked up.

"No," she answered. And for a moment I thought the collapsing inside would kill me.

No? No?

No.

On television shows this is the moment where there's a major blow up, and someone always storms out of the room. But the last thing I wanted to do was walk away from her. I loved her. I was stunned, and I wanted her to make sense of what I was experiencing. I wanted her to be with me far more than I wanted to claim the lame high ground of the victim. I didn't leave the table, never raised my voice, and took a long time before the snide jabs began. Mostly, I found myself using my begging voice, my wounded, sensitive-guy voice. The one I'm so self-conscious about. The one that makes me feel boring and safe and makes me wonder how much her choices are a reflection of my weakness.

She came back to my place after dinner. We ended up in my bedroom. She slipped out of her dress and stood before me in her black underwear and pearls. From the outset of our relationship, I've been completely intoxicated by her beauty and her body. She can do the splits against the wall standing up. She has a washboard stomach. There's this perfect tendon that traces inward from her hip. We spent our college years flirting with sex in a myriad of silly and even pathetic ways, and we both knew that after all that time, now that she had slept with him, she was about to sleep with me.

And that would be it. We were not going to survive as a couple. She wasn't going to choose between me and the other guy. She was going to keep moving forward with both of us in twisted ways, poisoning her options and forcing a response from him or from me until she made her choice without really ever making her choice; she would orchestrate what would happen to her and she would pay some weird penalty for her behaviors when he or I finally responded. She was stuck — painted into a corner — and she knew I knew it.

A better man would have sent her home in disgust. A lesser man would have taken her vigorously, selfishly, consuming something of her. I denied the obvious relational truth facing us, and hiding behind some lame and spineless rationalization about hope or romance, I stepped forward. And then she changed her mind. She shook as she put her dress back on. Here I cried. Here I begged. Here I took dirty shots. And then I repeated the process like it was a cheap shampoo, too weak the first time around, and enough to wound her the second. And then she was gone.

So she can wait while I eat my burrito and drink my stinking Mountain Dew on the sidewalk, a wino to my food on the street as a couple walks past, holding hands. I hate Chicago lovers.

I'm still on the sidewalk ten minutes later, wiping red chorizo oil from my hands with the paper bag, when Betsy gives up and arrives at the curb to hail a cab. She sees me and drops her shoulders.

"What are you doing?"

"Don't you recognize fine dining when you see it?"

"Didn't you see me waiting for you?"

"Do you think I usually take my meals on the sidewalk?" I answer her questions with questions because she hates it.

"Why are you avoiding me?"

"Uh, because you're sleeping with another guy?"

"Can we talk about it?"

"Will you quit sleeping with other guys?"

"Can we talk?"

"How about we go inside and even things up then, right now?"

"Please?"

"No? No? Hey — I didn't think you still used that word!"

"Don't do this." She's crying now. Again.

"You don't get to decide what I do anymore."

"I don't want to lose you." She's shaking. Again.

"Go home. I'm done with you," I say, and I know this immediate gratification will be followed by tearful apologies later. We both know it. We both know this is pure ugliness. And we both know we won't end well.

Betsy stops and stares. She inhales a sobbing, stuttering gasp. I am ice. Furious, venomous, profoundly hateful ice. She turns and runs with her hand over her mouth to Lake Shore to catch a taxi. I'm a complete wreck by the time I get to my apartment.

CHAPTER 3

TRUTH IN ADVERTISING

The drama with Betsy, and the gross feelings I've had about advertising in general, have me about ready to leave the agency, if I can muster the courage. In the year that I've been there, everything I've touched has turned to gold. I've been invited into every account the Chicago office has, and New York has asked for me on others. Fortune 50 giants and a host of pharmaceutical accounts make up the bulk of it. I hear from all sides how well things are going. The ultimate battle, though, is whether to believe what I hear or to admit the truth.

As I was leaving high school, my pastor took me aside and said, "I think you should consider the ministry. I believe you have a calling on your life." Such words don't come cheap in churches like mine, or from him. And there was something that felt true when he said it, like I already knew it somewhere. At the time, though, that was the last thing I wanted. A pastor? No way. Pastors drink tea with old ladies and have a creepy, fretting predilection for the health concerns of strangers. Not my deal. But the pastor's words haunted me anyway.

I spent my first two years at Indiana University taking prerequisite classes for IU's top-tier business school before switching to English when it became clear that my grades would fail to land me a job where I'd ever be chief officer of anything. I remember the walk home from an accounting exam fall semester of my sophomore year. I wasn't sure I'd passed, and rather than looking to the fact that I knew more about where Miller Lite was bottled than I did about FIFO, LIFO, or any other accounting principles, I negotiated for a loophole: "God, let me prove myself in the real world, and then you can have me." I mostly meant the prayer, but I didn't think about it again until recently.

When I graduated I sent letters and my lame portfolio to 125 agencies around the United States and the Caribbean. I got two interviews (both in Chicago, where Betsy had already assumed a position teaching high school algebra), and one job offer, which happened to come from the perfect place for me. At my agency there is none of the underdog attitude of a boutique shop. There is none of the creative bravado of a more artistic place. My agency is flat-out big, with big corporate clients and pure, soulless, results-based marketing agendas. It's been the perfect place to experience a sense of playing with the big boys, without the sense of yearning that comes in a smaller place, and none of the artistic elitism that congratulates people in other agencies. The circumstances of my employment, of my situation with my job, and with the results I've experienced here have simply been too perfect, and lately I find myself thinking of my prayer the day after that accounting test a lot. I'm beginning to see that I've been shown the end of an empty path, and that maybe I'm being drawn to something else. Something God has in mind.

There's an inherent immorality in advertising that shows itself in phrases like "create a need." Novelist Booth Tarkington once wrote that "the voice of the people is the voice of their god," and in America nothing impacts the voice of the people like advertising. That's the way it is, but nobody creating a god, or an idol, can do so without eventually feeling some deep internal conflict. It feels wrong to scare the collector crabs into scrambling for extra camouflage or shiny bits. Likewise, there is something inherently immoral about using a gift or ability for the good of something you don't believe in. It's a prostitution, really, and people in advertising talk about it all the time. The more I consider my job, the more these truths about the immorality of it all strike home. And the more they strike home, the more I think about my prayer after the accounting test.

Then, last week, along comes the perfect last-straw account, gift-wrapped and too clearly wrong to not be from God, it seems. The new product is a spermicidal gel that adds less than one percent to the efficacy of birth control. As far as I can tell from the data available to me, it's a nearly worthless product. Plus, they want to market it to teenagers. So if I do my job well, I'll help derail the lives of kids who are no match for the power of my message and my thinly veiled invitation to foolish, sinful choices. Not everyone is offered such a clear-cut opportunity to choose the right path, and the clarity of it makes me think about the second half of my prayer that day on my way back to my dorm room after the accounting test — the part about "then you can have me." I know, deep down, that the truth of my success is that God let me walk with my idol until I could see it well enough to put it down and head in the other direction.

I don't know how the word is used in the Bible, but to my marketing mind an idol is a god you can put in your pocket. It's something you can control, pull out when you need a dose of insurance or magic, and then put away while things click along well. Oh, and an idol will always choose your death over its own. This is true of careers, relationships, doctrines, fears, hiding places, and even the choices we make to "believe in ourselves." Even the idol of me will choose my death over its own. It happens with suicide, but it also happens in a million living ways too. We die in favor of the idols of ourselves anytime we can't admit the truth to ourselves. And we're all addicts to that one, I'm afraid.

Idols are good for two things: making us feel important and making us feel loved. Importance and love are good things, but you know they've become idols when the evidence of importance or adoration is something you try to control yourself. My job makes me feel important, and I work hard to prove how important it makes me. Ask my cab drivers or the friends and family who get to hear me drop names or brag in cocky, matter-of-fact tones. And when I feel important, I feel as though it is right for others to love me. And when I feel I understand what makes people love me, then I feel a control over that love.

The whole deal is sick, and my environment is only making matters worse. I need to make some serious changes, if I can make myself pull the trigger.

It's midafternoon, and I've been waiting all day to talk to my boss, Buzz. Catching him will be easy; he has to step through my office to get to his — his being the corner office and mine being one that was originally designed for a secretary to the guy in the corner office. He created a rule that I'm not allowed to close his door or "alter the conditions" of his office. He's been gone in meetings all day, but he likes to return to the same setting as he left, so he hit "repeat" on his CD player. For almost three hours I've been listening to Ted Nugent's "Stranglehold" while the smell of baking yeast wafts its way into my office from the bread maker on his windowsill.

What makes Buzz especially fascinating to me is the way he uses the word "should." I was taught not to use it because "should" is "too bossy," but he uses it in an intimate way and works the word as the lynchpin to moments where he claims an authority over someone else's world — always their personal world. When he says, "You should do that," most people do. They call their mothers. They have another drink. They sleep with people from the office. I've even been trying to take up smoking because of Buzz, because he said I should, because, "It's cool — especially the menthols." Buzz has an idol's sort of power over people. They trust him and give him more power, and he makes them feel important and loved, sort of. When it's used well, "should" can be as potent as my use of "they," which is a great word for telling lies:

"*They* told me inside that I wouldn't have to pay for parking."

"They did?"

"Yes."

"Okay, if they say so."

"Thanks. Have a great day."

In many ways, my boss and I are birds of a twisted feather, and I know that two things will be certain when I tell him about my plans to leave: he'll be hurt enough to try to keep me, and then he'll be angry enough to bludgeon me and completely burn the relationship if I reject his efforts to keep me. The fact that our talk is coming two days after he decorated my office for my birthday doesn't help.

There is a game of Frisbee going on in the hallway when Buzz returns from his meetings, and he joins in for a couple of tosses, pushing the limits and adding some wrinkle to the game that I can't understand from where I'm sitting. He's wearing jeans, a gray dress shirt, and sneakers in which he always walks buoyantly on the balls of his feet. He's athletic the way someone who could have played sports but chose the drama club instead is athletic. Julie, the gorgeous art school intern, wanders into the hall and tells him how great the bread smells. He invites everyone to come grab a slice.

The party moves into and through my office to his, and then spreads into both. He's perfect for his job because he's just a little *more* of everything than everyone around him. He's a little more devious, a little more disciplined, a little more curious, a little more insightful, a little more seasoned, a little more gifted, a little more connected, a little more aware of where everyone's careers and lives are heading. It's all part of a well-crafted persona — the persona that lets him use the word "should."

I stick to my work, making only small talk with the bread munchers. I'm trying to be rude, trying to make sure they feel like intruders and hurry through. I'm the wet blanket. I rifle loudly through my metal desk drawer to find my headphones and plug them into my stereo. At one point Buzz makes a face and a palms-up gesture to ask if I'm okay. I respond with a gesture that I'm busy and my shaking vertical fingers complain about the chaos he's creating with all of these people. Half an hour later everyone's gone and Buzz is back to work in his office. And then, after all of my previous eagerness, I don't move. I listen to my mix tape and drown myself in Pearl Jam and Urge Overkill, not at all eager to quit my job.

Is this really what I want to do? Is this God's leading, or is this me guessing what God would say? Am I making God my imaginary friend and playing the roles of us both? Is this me running away from success? Fearing failure? Is this my inability to stand the pain of my ordinary world, suddenly in shambles with all the junk going on with Betsy? What else will I do? If God wants me, where does he want me? It must involve the skills I've gained in advertising, right? He wouldn't just throw away the time, would he? A whole year? What might he want me to do instead? Advertising is all about creating a need, and the only need people really have is him, so maybe what

he wants is for me to create marketing materials that help people feel their need for God. Maybe? Maybe shape the voice of the people to speak of a true God?

And then what, send them to church? Right. I don't get church. It was fine for high school cutesy stuff, but I have no idea why adults attend, except that it's what they feel like they're supposed to do. It's another "should" argued by people who have been told by some nameless "them" that this is how God wants things. It's just a holy rubber stamp, and it's more fake than any beer commercial could ever be. A leftover tradition. A group fantasy. A dead end. I'd feel better about selling motherhood to a teenager than church to a person looking for God. At least the God I know.

The God I know is not the God who wants to hear a prayer of confession read from a program. The God I believe in cares about real lives. He makes use of talents — he even gives us those talents in the first place. The people my God would point to as heroes are not the weirdos hiding in churches, but the people who actually do something because they believe in him and care about the things he says to care about. The God I believe in will experience tremendous grief with each soul consumed by the fires of hell, even if the church people clap and dance and giggle with each sizzle and pop. He would choose to be known. He would choose to love and be loved. He would choose to be chosen. He will serve up a major smack down for church people who become barriers to people who seek him more honestly. He will have little patience with the church people who have not shown mercy to sinners, who have stepped over their brother on the street, who have lied to them and made them feel uninvited until they got their worlds in order. The God I believe in will punish people whose "good, healthy boundaries" are not based in truth and love, but in selfish, gluttonous security and safety rather than faith, and who would let their sister bleed to death before they'd let her bleed on their new carpet. No, I don't want to send people to church.

I've been reading about Habitat for Humanity, and I've seen stuff on television about some big men's ministry that has rallies in football arenas. What if the two groups could get together for a week or two — a million men swinging hammers across the country to do something helpful for thousands of people with little other proof that Christianity is real to the people who profess it? I can see people watching TV at the corner bar noticing the news article about that one. They'd have to admit that for whatever else a person may say about the people of God, Christians do make a difference and do display acts of loving generosity. That's a "brand" people would join, would want to be associated with, would use to tell themselves and others the story of who they are. That would be a need worth creating, worth pointing out, worth creating a hunger for. Maybe that's something God would have me do?

Or at least stuff like that. There are all sorts of places where Christians are doing good things, where people's needs are being met by Christians who offer their services in the name of Jesus. Maybe all the church needs is a new way of being seen, a new way of expressing itself. A new and better PR campaign.

4:07. I still haven't moved. Then Russ Taff's song "I Still Believe" comes on my stereo headphones, and I have *a moment* — time stops, angels sing their dramatic "ah-ee-ah," and I know what's next. I do still believe. And more than that, I *want* to believe. It is true that my world is a mess. It is true that things with my job are going well, apart from the crisis of conscience. It is true that I have no idea what I'd do, or any idea how well I'd do, or any clear sense that the Habitat for Humanity idea has any potential. It is true that I am not a church person — and I certainly don't talk like one anymore. It is true that I am about to commit professional suicide. But in the face of all that, some things are even more true, and they boil down to the fact that I *want* God to have been calling me all my life. I *want* there to be more than money, flashy work, and lying to cab drivers. I *want* this whole God thing to be real. I *want* William Blake to have been right when he wrote about there being more than our five senses. I *want* to know a truth that transcends the system, that transcends the truth I already know. I *want* to be about something more. I *want* to believe, and I want it to show. Freakin' Russ Taff. I rise from my chair, and I know that I am about to choose an entirely different path for the rest of my life. Right now. Right now. Everything changes, right now. My world's apocalypse, right now.

I feel like I've just stood up in a giant lecture hall and screamed, "Liar!" at the professor. All eyes are on me, and my words are distant — I can't hear them and I can't tell if I'm making any sense. I'm just flowing, clumsy and flush with adrenaline.

"Buzz? Got a minute?"

CHAPTER 4

Bravado Runs Away

"I don't know what's happening to me, David." I'm sobbing into the phone with the sort of gusto men allow each other only once in their relationships. "Everything is falling apart, and I don't know if I can handle it."

David has been my best friend for years. We were in youth group together. He's two years older and is at seminary in Denver. He got married three months ago. Our mutual friend and I flew in for the wedding together. We thought we were pretty cool, coming from the big city ready for a bachelor party and a weekend of drinking with the seminarian we hoped to get drunk at the strip club. Excitement in David's world looked more than a bit different; he picked us up at the airport and couldn't wait to tell us how he'd made it all the way from Denver Seminary to Stapleton International without having to stop for a light. The bachelor party turned out to be a campfire in the mountains with a group of guys. One of them even brought a veggie platter. The only nudity was a cupcake with boobs on the top, which competed with the cigars and one beer apiece for the most debauched part of the night. But that was three months ago; tonight there is a sweeping drama unfolding and David was the guy who picked up the phone to hear about it.

"I feel totally adrift," I blather.

"I bet." David is working on his Masters of Divinity in counseling and is diligent about practicing his active listening. "It must be hard for you."

"It has been. Buzz's boss told me she'd miss watching my career. She said that with everyone else in the agency she could tell how far they'd go, but she didn't see a ceiling for me and had been looking forward to what I'd do. I know she was probably just doing the white-bread praise thing, but it felt good, you know?"

"That's really cool. And I'm sure she wouldn't say it if it wasn't at least partly true."

"I don't know. The whole job drama is just part of it anyway. I'm totally twisted up about Betsy, and I know it's crazy, but I feel like I'm being attacked spiritually, like demons and stuff. I can't sleep. I'm afraid that someone's going to break through the window from the fire escape. Everything feels chaotic and frightening. I don't know who I am, and I don't know where I'm going, and I can't believe I made this choice because I wanted to do public relations for *God*. What is that?"

"It's not crazy. There is a spiritual world, and you've just made a choice that makes you show up on the radar of a war that's going on. You're stepping out in response to God. That's going to make you some enemies."

"I made one with Buzz today. I told him I wasn't going to take the offer he made. It was so weird the way we left things last night too. We were at the corner in front of that place where I took you to lunch when you were here, and the streets were empty, no people and no cars. There was fog and the streets were wet. It totally felt like a meeting outside of time. The orange flashing of the Don't Walk lights and the green from the traffic signal were in the puddles, and I felt like I was making the choice they represented — that there was a green light to go forward, and a warning not to go any further with him. I said goodbye at the corner and walked north a block before I got a cab. It was creepy, like there were angels and demons around us or something."

"So what happened today when you told him, then?"

"He told me that he hoped I knew that he would never give me a recommendation and that he didn't ever want to talk to me again, and that I should leave the building immediately."

"That had to be hard after how close you've felt to him."

"Yeah, it was. It wasn't a surprise, but I hadn't thought about how much it would hurt."

"And you're not someone who deals well with having people mad at you."

"I guess. It was just so sudden, even though I knew the end was coming. I stuck my head in a few offices on my way out and told those people what had happened, and that I was on my way out right then. No real goodbyes at all."

"Man."

"But here's the part that really got me." I have to take a minute because I start crying too hard again. I blow my nose on my shirt and continue. "Diane, the office manager who's spent six months of weekly lunches telling me about her marriage being in trouble, was one of the people who was in her office on my way out. She knew I was leaving, but asked me to tell her again why I was going. I told her about the Christian PR thing, about Habitat and — I told you about that idea, didn't I?"

"Yeah. Has Habitat responded to your letter yet?"

"No, they haven't. But today, when I told her about it, her response was 'Huh, I didn't know you were a Christian.'"

"Oh, ouch."

"I've spent a year with this person, and I've spent six months in intimate confidence with her, and after all that time and all that depth I'd never given her a noticeable clue about me and God. I thought I was being 'salt' in the agency. I thought I was being some sort of example or witness or whatever, and she had no idea. And so now here I am, walking away from the industry with all these bad feelings about it, and about my part in it, with my boss cursing me, and it feels like a complete waste because I don't even get the caveat of, 'At least I was a visible Christian who did a great job before he left.' I have no credibility, and this whole thing about doing work for God must sound like it's coming completely from right field to them. I've spent a year as a total sellout, and I have nothing to show for it."

"A chasing after the wind."

"What?"

"It's from Ecclesiastes."

"And I don't know a thing about the Bible, either, it seems."

"I think you need to get away. Get on a plane and come spend a long weekend with us. You're too close to the mess, and you're torturing yourself with everything. If it's God calling you, your best bet is to get away where you can be still and know he is God."

"Is that Scripture too?"

"Psalm 46:10."

"Do you have the whole thing memorized or something?"

"No, just the popular ones on the cheesy art from the Christian bookstores."

"Do they really have special bookstores now?"

"You should come out this weekend. We don't have to go to a Christian bookstore, but it would be good for you. Getting away, I mean."

CHAPTER 5

Confessions of a Nice Guy

I spent five days in Denver with David and his wife Danielle, and decided to move there. David's father-in-law took me fly fishing on the Poudre River outside of Fort Collins, and the lazy dozing I did on a sun-warmed rock in the river was the first time I've ever been fully present, both in location and time. I wasn't daydreaming about being anyplace else, and I wasn't reviewing my list of what makes me good or not good or whatever, and I didn't feel fat or smart or lost or like I needed to prove myself or anything. I just felt the rush of water, the warmth of sunlight, and the joy of being completely unplugged from my normal world. It felt like peace. I want more of it.

I've returned to Chicago for my things and to say my goodbyes. My lease runs through the end of September, which is perfect, and I think again about the agreement God and I made after my accounting test, and how all of the details are working out so that all of my potential excuses to back out on things with God are being cleared from my path.

It's my first night back in town. Betsy and I lie on the pale blue carpet of her apartment and let the evening fade to night. The streetlight dapples the room through tree branches and the wavy glass of the windows. We listen to the sound of people on the street below, heading to the bars, and we let the Band-Aid pull from our hearts slowly, exquisitely. We cry. We kiss. We talk. We hold each other, and we open our hands to the years and dreams we've had together, letting them slip into the current of life around us. Our time together drifts away, sinking. It feels so grown-up, so sad, like a movie from the seventies. College is really over now, and in the chill of the real world, so is our relationship.

I don't know if it has to be this way. I don't know why she's been with the other guy. I want to ask, but the whole subject is too loaded, too volatile for both of us, so I just lay my ear on the warm skin of her stomach and watch her chin move as she whispers to me. The wound she has inflicted is profound, but she is tender toward me, and somewhere in my heart I conclude that she doesn't know why this is happening either. I will take the trade, the pain for its gentle delivery, and I will be okay.

Besides, there is Denver. There is a whole new adventure coming. I still haven't heard from Habitat for Humanity regarding my idea, but that's up to God anyway. David said it's my job to provide the momentum; God will provide the direction. And maybe his plan still involves Betsy. Maybe if I succeed at this, if I can learn to be more exciting, without becoming a workaholic; if I can bring in a great salary; if my prayers wake something up in Betsy; if I lose some weight; maybe if I learn to ski, even. Who knows? It's a whole new world. And we do have a history together. God wouldn't throw away four-and-a-half years, would he? God redeems some idols, doesn't he?

For nice guys there is always a list of maybes. Nothing is ever exactly in a nice guy's control, because everything comes as a response to the bait or display with which he lures the objects of his desire. It's never overtly about him; and with that comes a tremendous sense of insecurity because everything about a nice guy is derivative, contingent upon the response he can manipulate.

Here's the thing about the sensitive voice, the fearful regret of playing the nice guy, the worry that I am too boring or safe: this role has been my salvation for most of my life, and I don't know what else there is to me. I can do the cocky thing, and I do play that role, but it comes from an insincere and frightened place. It comes because I'm a doormat with no place for my frustrations to go, except Burritoville. I'm clumsy with anything but the doormat role, but being the nice guy is a dishonest persona; it's not who I am. I'm stuck there, hiding my inconsistencies in places that feel impenetrable to me, but I know they're plain to anyone who bothers to look. I live on the social meniscus that is the unspoken promise to politely ignore each other's foibles. I fear the breaking of that meniscus, and what would happen to me, and I hate living in that fear. That's the catch with camouflaged hiding places, I guess — they're more prison than protection, locking you away until the day they fail you.

When I was a senior in high school, I dated a girl from my youth group who went to a different school. At my school I was known as the guy who kept a count on how many days he'd been dating his girlfriend, who would leave roses on her doorstep and ran away in case she didn't feel presentable. I was the guy who left notes on her car, who once pulled alongside the school bus in which her marching band was traveling with a sign asking if people could believe how cute she was. I did the things that made the girls in my high school gush, though it got to a point where my girlfriend asked me to lay off on the flowers. It may not have been overt, but it was all about me. I'd stumbled onto a way to seem desirable without having to be great looking. I offered tribute at the feet of my idol — which was not the girl, but the pile of evidence for what a great guy I was — and the idol gave me a sense of control over my lovableness. I discovered the bribery of apparent love and assured service — and for years it's worked. During my senior year of high school, I had "friend dates," afternoon outings of bowling or pool or movies or a walk through the park, with maybe forty girls from my school. I was the nice guy. And sometimes we'd make out.

I'm thinking about this as Betsy and I lie on the floor of her apartment, saying goodbye and feeling full of emotions, feeling tortured about the end, though part of me is quite interested in one last effort at coitus. Somewhere along the line the selfish, un-nice idol worshipper in me learned to hide my reasons for abstinence behind her reasons, and now we've come to a place where neither of us has spoken about the truth for over a year.

My girlfriend was still in high school when I left for college. It was my freshman year, and I'd begun my intensive study of Miller Lite. On Fridays everyone from the floor of the dorm where I lived would gather in my neighbor's room at noon, beer in hand, and we'd play Jimi Hendrix's version of "The Star-Spangled Banner" from Woodstock, and then crack open the beers and begin the weekend. We'd drink all afternoon and all evening until we all pretty much passed out. It was a tradition with which we were quite impressed. I still have a photo from that day in which I'm wearing a blue-and-black plaid flannel shirt, open over a white T-shirt. I'm also wrapped in a long ribbon of white trash bags I stole from the janitor's closet. The bags are tied around me like a toga, then knotted in a giant bow on my forehead. In the photo I'm holding a 32-ounce Hardee's cup in a salute, and smiling for the camera about the way I guess I'd expect somebody drunk and wrapped in trash bags to smile.

I finished my twenty-third beer somewhere around eleven o'clock that evening. When I spilled on my flannel shirt, I returned to my room to change into another one. The place was full of my room-mate's friends, including a girl named Melissa. I'd seen her around, and I knew she was a hometown friend of the bald guy across the hall we all called Mr. Clean. She'd been drinking too. I was between flannels, at my open closet, when she approached me.

"You know, I've always found you attractive," she said, putting her hand on my chest.

I made the motorboat sound with my lips in a laughing re-sponse to the moment and to her approach. And to her. Sexy. Classy. Suave.

I remember being led to the beanbag chair. I remember her put-ting my roommate's cowboy hat on me. I remember my roommate and his girlfriend ushering people out of the room. I remember the condom package my roommate tossed at me landing on my shoulder. I remember talking. I remember her crying about her father, who left the family to sell time-shares in Cancun. I remember Kate Bush on the stereo. And that's all I remember.

Before I woke up I could tell someone was beside me, right by my face on the top bunk. It was my roommate and his girlfriend, grinning and teasing me out of my sleep. Melissa was gone, and for a moment I didn't remember what had happened, or at least hoped it had been a dream somehow.

"Tell me — " I began to ask, but they pulled apart and gestured to Melissa's bra, which they'd spread on the back of the chair. Then they scurried out of the room to tell all of the guys on the hall.

I was heartbroken. I was absolutely disappointed in myself. I wanted so desperately to escape the fact of what I had done, but of course with such moments, or with any sin considered honestly, there is no escape. It was there, and so was the reflection of my failure. I had a ferocious hangover, and the tearing inside my heart joined right in. I spent the first morning of some portion of my soul's honeymoon dry heaving into the dorm toilet where someone else had previously done likewise, with horrendous aim. By the time I returned to my room there was a group of guys standing by my door, to which they had already applied a handmade "Player of the Week" poster with Melissa's bra thumbtacked to it. I cut the bra up and put it in the garbage. By the next morning, the poster had moved to someone else's door.

The desire to find a loophole for what I'd done was overwhelming. I hadn't pursued it, and a case could be made that I was in no condition to make such choices. I tried out the date rape line of logic on one of the guys from the hall. It didn't fly at all. Still, I was incredibly angry with Melissa. I felt like she'd stolen something from me. I saw her as a reminder of my failure, and I wanted to have nothing to do with her. She knocked on my door the next night after I'd gone to sleep. I opened it a few inches without getting out of bed. She asked if she could take my picture. It may still exist somewhere — me with messy hair and an angry, guilty, icy stare. Then she asked if I had her bra. I told her I'd thrown it away, which of course I knew would hurt her, but not as badly as the whole truth. After that, I never spoke with her again, except once toward the end of our senior year when I passed her between classes and said hello.

There was no loophole, but I was determined to keep the failure from touching me. It did not fit with the way I thought of myself or the evidence I relied upon to describe myself. I prayed. I repented. I cried. And I swore to God that I would not have sex again until it was with my wife. I told Betsy about all of this, and as our relationship was growing, that promise started out being the thing that stopped us. It fit nicely into the fear and guilt she'd learned growing up Catholic. And somewhere I'm certain that I taught her she would bear part of the responsibility for my breaking a promise to God if we let things go all the way. It was easier to tell friends, coworkers, and even myself that she was the reason we were holding off, but it was more my thing, even if I'd weakened so much that she was the only one keeping the promise anymore.

Now we find ourselves five years later, curled up on the floor, skin on skin, soft kisses and broken hearts, with my promise kept in spite of myself, and both of us more than a bit confused by the whole experience.

How much of the time does it work that way with God? How much of the time does he orchestrate the keeping of the covenants we make with him? Is the promise of a fallen man worth anything at all? There were times where Betsy wanted to, asked to, and I refused. And there were plenty of times when the reverse was the case. My promise has been fleeting and forgotten and flat-out fought against. It was worth nothing, when kiss came to tug. Still, we haven't physically broken it. Is that God intervening somehow? Is that some sort of mercy from him, something protecting me from feeling double the despair I felt the morning after Melissa, or from learning to ignore the disappointment altogether? Is it help from him to stick to a wiser game plan? Is it him showing me that I can only keep promises with his help? Is it him telling me how foolish it is to make or trust promises at all? Or maybe it's him saying that the only promises I should make are ones that include him in their keeping? Or maybe this whole five-year flirtation with temptation has all been in my head, and the internal and relational junk has all been inflicted by my Protestant performance-oriented faith. Maybe if we'd been intimate the whole time we both would have invested more, would have had some different kind of balance in our worlds, would have stuffed less down, and wouldn't be avoiding conversations about a sex life we don't share. Maybe if we'd been freer, we wouldn't be lying here right now, letting it all go.

This is what the "nice guy" thing gets me. This is why the sensitive voice scares me, and why safety and trustworthiness seem like such meaningless traits. I can't control how things turn out, and I'm not giving other people honest information about myself with which to draw conclusions. The facts are different from the façade. I'm not safe. I'm not trustworthy. I'm not sensitive or nice. I'm the guy who had a one-night stand with someone he then shunned, who soon thereafter broke up with the girl to whom he'd never been exactly loyal or disloyal until the one-night stand, and who then spent five years twisting the next girl into the convoluted rules and logic he'd come up with in his wrestling match between the vague heavens of which he dreamed himself worthy, and the all-too concrete damnation to which he suspected himself wed.

Still, here I am playing victim and claiming some high road when Betsy tells me about another guy. I'm the one who cried when I noticed the condom wrapper in the bathroom. She'd be shocked to know the truth about what really goes on inside of me, about how much like her I really am. I'm supposed to be the nice guy, the safe guy, the trustworthy guy with the inescapable conscience. I'm the guy she's wounded so, so deeply and will forever feel guilty about; the one spinning out of control and moving away; the one gently beside her, feeling the depth and the gravity of the end of our time together. It's all an exaggerated and false self — I'd sleep with her right now if she would. I'm not sensitive; I'm cowardly. And the absurd, identity-splitting denials that remain dedicated to the idol of myself merely prove to me that it's all more than I'm able to let sink in.

CHAPTER 6

LEAVING MAYBERRY

Two days later I'm in the Indianapolis suburbs, passing through my parents' place on my way to Denver. There have been questions and concerns, and both my pastor and a woman I've never met have asked for time together before I head west.

The pastor and I meet for lunch at the Friendly Tavern on Zionsville's cobbled Main Street. Glenn is the one who told me to consider the ministry when I was in high school. I prayed "the prayer" for salvation in the bed next to his when I was fifteen and we were heading to a work project in Juarez, Mexico. I have a framed 8 x 10 photo from that trip with all of the kids from the youth group standing in a trench we'd dug for the foundation of a church addition, and Glenn is beside the trench with a shovel and a canister of grape Kool-Aid; part of his alter ego from the trip, the Reverend Biff Jones.

"What do your parents think?" he asks.

"They think I'm nuts," I answer.

"Probably not a surprise."

"Do you think I'm nuts too?"

"No. I think God is drawing you out of your ordinary world." He sips his Mountain Dew. "But you have to understand how challenging all of this will be to them. And to you, for that matter. This is not part of the plan any of you had in mind, and it breaks all of the rules."

"I don't know that it does. It's not like I'm going off to live in some rat hole in Calcutta."

"Not that you know of." He's toying with me, skirting way too near to the whole limp-wristed pastoral image for me.

"No, I'm pretty sure about that. Besides, I can probably do the PR-for-God stuff on the side, if I have to. I don't see any reason I have to be poor to be obedient."

He grins a little bit like he doesn't believe me, and then asks, "So, you've told me what you'd like to do, but you haven't told me why."

"Good question," I say, intending the arrogance. I think it's obvious that the Church has been failing in managing its reputation, and that he's part of it. In selling, or in pitching agency services, this is called the "probe and disturb" portion of the program. "I think the Church has become a toothless lion. And the teeth have been pulled by church people who don't really believe what they say they believe. They don't serve the people they say they've been called to serve; they don't trust the truths they say they trust; they don't love the people they say they love; they don't keep the promises they say they'll keep; and they don't point to the sort of God they say they point to. People from within the Church have made errors in judgment, like the televangelists, and those errors have diminished the Church's credibility; and the more that credibility has been diminished, the more people within the Church have capitulated with society's efforts to relegate the Church to some quaint, outmoded superstition; and the more that has happened, the more the Church has been left with little to show for itself but the arcane bromides of its small, dark existence."

Glenn grins doubtfully again. "I think we'd probably describe things a bit differently, but I understand what you're looking at. And you've already told me some of how you'd envision addressing the problems. But why do you want to give your life to addressing them?"

"Well, right now it's still just an idea. I don't know that I necessarily want to spend my life addressing the public perception issues of the Church."

"Let's say you had drawn that conclusion. What's the desire in your heart that you'd be addressing?"

"God is real. I've felt him. I've known life paying attention to him and life ignoring him — and I know that life paying attention is better. I also know the Church was his idea, and for however messed up it is, it must be the best vehicle for his purposes. I'd like to show non-Christians something about life with God being better than life without him, so they could also experience it. And for people in the Church, in this God-designed vehicle, I'd like to be a part of helping them get back in touch with the incredible power and potential of the Church; of the Church when it spends its life paying attention to God."

"So what's in it for you is the satisfaction of helping other people experience God?"

"Yes. And it would be great to be a part of reshaping church so that it was a place that made sense for me, and people like me. Maybe that's what I really want to find — a sort of Christianity that fits me."

"Yeah, that's a big one. I think we're all after that. Would it be fair to say that the root of what you're after is the changing of lives — a bunch of lives?"

"Ultimately, yes. Though the first step is shifting some perceptions and redefining the Christian 'brand.'"

Glenn pops a couple of ketchup-laden fries into his mouth, nodding with a thoughtful grunt.

"What are you thinking?" I ask.

"I think you may be working with unsatisfying tools."

"Huh?"

"If your desire is to change lives, and you want to change the culture of the Church to find a place for yourself in it, I think you may be disappointed going the route you're talking about." He folds his napkin beneath the lip of his plate. "Nobody has ever become a disciple of Christ through impersonal means. You may see hundreds of people come down front in an altar call at a Billy Graham event, but that's just the first step. What is always necessary, at least in my experience, is another person, a relationship in which the new believer can learn and ask questions and experience love. If what you're wanting to see is a change in lives and in the Church, I don't think you'll see it with mass media." He studies me for a moment. "And if it makes you feel any better, delivering a sermon usually feels about as impersonal and ineffective as mass media."

This, of course, is a load of garbage. This is Glenn having given up on telling the truth, and instead telling only the stories that sell in church. You can't tell me people won't buy God if the Church decides it actually cares about moving its product.

"Thanks, Glenn. That's a lot to think about. I hope you're wrong, but I'm eager to find out for myself. Thanks for lunch too."

"I'll be praying for you," he answers. I know he means it, which feels good, for whatever that's worth.

We say our goodbyes and head to our cars. I drive past the cutesy shops of Main Street, through the Victorian part of town people call the Village, and out past the football stadium the school built after our first state championship. Zionsville has been my hometown since my freshman year of high school. It's affluent, Anglo, and has to be as homogenized as any place on Earth. It's a bedroom community, populated largely by employees of the pharmaceutical giant Eli Lilly and Company, the makers of Prozac. The company transfers families in and out of town all the time. On my first day at the school I was asked repeatedly if I was a "Lilly Kid," and everyone knows who's meant by the term "Uncle Eli." The existence of Zionsville, with its gazebos and parks and Mayberry charms — its undying desire for a bit of idyllic Heaven on Earth — is proof to me that we have a collective memory of Eden. Zionsville's proximity to, and utter disregard for, the poverty, crime, and abuses found beyond its gates is proof to me that there was a reason we were kicked out of the garden.

My parents are at home in Zionsville. Dad's the dutiful Lilly executive, and Mom's a fine, nurturing housewife. Both are secure and polite and apparently in full agreement with the rationalizations embraced by the community of which they are a part. My choices have them at a complete loss. Mom is indeed a warm and caring, loyal and insightful woman of indefatigable sacrificial nature, and Dad is truly remarkable for his abilities, discipline, wisdom, and ability to wield power. Both are wholly sincere. They brought their 1950s North Dakota worldview with them as they raised me and my two younger brothers, climbed the corporate ladder, and weathered the storms common to most marriages. I think their parents would be very proud of them. They have lived the American Dream, at least the one articulated by the "Haves" to the "Would Like to Haves" for generations. They have worked hard, invested well, and dream of a nice long retirement.

There was a time when my mother was reading the police blotter in the local paper and saw my friend's name there. "I'm glad that's not my kid," she said, meaning how embarrassing it would be and how people may think her a bad mother if our family experienced similar problems. Not to worry, though; she raised three good boys. Nice guys, with sensitive guy voices.

Mom's terrified, which she'd say is the appropriate response when one's eldest son quits his job and decides to move across the country with no housing lined up to do who-knows-what, especially right as a four-plus-year relationship with a perfectly nice, polite, very presentable girl is being thrown away.

Dad thinks I'm a fool, which is about as easy a conclusion to reach as the one my mother uncovered. I've tried to explain, but I have to give them room for their opinions. I sure can't make a great case for what I'm doing either, at least not without falling back to the whole prayer to God after the accounting test story, and while my parents have been active at church for years, they simply do not do things "because God said so." Ever. So far the closest thing Dad's come to support, which also seems to be his final word on the subject, is, "I guess you gotta do what you gotta do."

In Zionsville, my father's ways sure seem like the facts of life. His way has worked; there's no getting around that. I'm twenty-three, and I know that means I have a lot to learn. But man, do I hope it doesn't turn out he and Zionsville have been right about relationships and careers and priorities all along. If Zionsville has things right, I'm heading in exactly the wrong direction.

It's Sunday morning and I'm supposed to meet some woman named Ivy in the church parlor. She called and said she wanted to talk about my career choices. Of course I assumed that she heard about what's happening through the incredibly efficient Zionsville Presbyterian Aunt Bee network. Mom says she didn't say a word. I've heard of Ivy before. Big money. Far-flung network. Passion about influencing media. Not a particularly gifted people pleaser. In fact, I remember someone whose midwestern wifely feathers she'd ruffled referring to her as a "witch for Jesus."

So that's who I watch for as I wait in the parlor, sitting amid the uncomfortable granny furniture, not certain that I'm allowed to be drinking lemonade in this room. Ivy enters, and I'm suddenly scared. Think German schoolmarm. With tenure. And a penchant for corporal punishment. From our brief phone conversation, and what I've heard from other people, I know she's extremely matter-of-fact, very blunt, and it's clear she doesn't see the utility in humor. Such, I guess, is the prerogative of wealthy people in a culture where money is so often confused with power and credibility, and where weak people invite rich people to be bullies.

"You need to return to Chicago and stay in advertising. That is what God would have you do."

I start to explain that I've already left. I start to explain that the industry is immoral. I start to explain about Habitat for Humanity.

"No. Your job is to perform in the advertising world, rise as far as you can, and affect change from there. I've been watching you since you were writing for the high school newspaper, and this is simply what you're meant to do. Anything else is a waste of the life God's given you."

I tell her that I'm interested in finding a parallel track, maybe a Christian advertising agency.

"No. You are meant to be a healthy cell in an otherwise cancerous body. You are not meant to drop out and be a part of the Christian subculture. You are meant to impact the general culture."

I tell her I don't want to be a part of the Christian subculture. Then I ask what about the network TV shows she's funded? Did those efforts reach beyond the Christian subculture? I tell her I want to show a more real, more desirable faith. I want to stand for the right things. I tell her I don't know exactly what this will look like, yet, but that I do know it doesn't include going back to Chicago.

She tells me about William Wilberforce's protracted, but ultimately successful, efforts to end slavery in England. She tells me we are in a similar battle. She tells me that she's funded some very highly rated shows, and that they offer a far superior alternative to the other stuff on television. She tells me that the more people produce shows of moral character, the more that will influence the culture, the same way negative shows undermine the culture. She tells me that it is my duty to do the same thing in the advertising world.

I picture blurry-edged soup commercials and sentimental coffee ads. So what? Who cares about that? Then I picture being a Bible thumper back at the agency in Chicago. She has no idea what the place was like. She has no idea how readily it consumed me — and how much I let it. I am not a role model, and there's no way I see myself spending a career building some external "witness" so I can push for less sex in the Shedd's Spread campaign. I'm confused about my options, but I know I need to be explicitly about God.

I ask her what she thinks about Glenn's comments — about the relative value of mass media and interpersonal communication. She tells me that all interpersonal communication happens within a context, and that the single most powerful voice in the shaping of that context, at least in America, is the combined voice of mass media. She says that Glenn may be right in terms of the reaping, but that my calling has everything to do with sowing, and that my job is to shape a context in which truth and love and community are properly understood and valued. And then, before I can ask or say another thing, she tells me that our time is up, rises, shakes my hand, and leaves me alone with my lemonade.

CHAPTER 7

For Those About to Rock

I leave Zionsville wearing my leather cowboy-ish fishing hat, feeling very much like a man heading for the mountains. That lasts until the middle of Illinois, the tin box dashboard radio turned up enough to screech over the sound of a barely functional truck the rental place had to be glad to get rid of. I sing. I cry. I sing and cry. I figure Betsy will be home and pull over to call her from a pay phone. No answer. I stop to try again every hundred miles or so until just after two o'clock this morning, west of Topeka, when I finally realize she's at the other guy's place.

So that's that.

But I have more pressing matters to consider right now. Outside it's pitch black and raining. Really raining. And windy. I've had slow to about forty miles an hour a couple of times, and I've not that even a fully loaded Ryder truck can hydroplane. P *right* about to stop. I've turned the radio up even further - *he rain* now — to keep me awake and to compete with th' 57 and the wipers. The nasty crosswind and the lousy visibility and the emotions and the lack of sleep and the loud music grating its way through the blown speakers pile on and make this as white-knuckled as things get.

I'm terrified. I may well die on the road tonight; I'm getting pushed all over the place and am spending half my time on the rumble strips. Everything in the world says to stop, to turn back. Betsy asked me to reconsider. My parents are against this. Glenn and Ivy both think I'm being a fool. A few minutes ago there was a tornado warning on the radio — but I don't know what county I'm in so the warning didn't do me any good and I've kept going. My brain wants me to turn around, to call this off. I really have nothing to gain, and besides, I only have one year of professional experience. Who cares how well it went? It won't be worth anything to anyone in the real world. What the heck am I doing? Why am I doing this? What if this really is just about my embarrassment, and I'm running away like my dad says? Maybe I should head home. The tears start again. And then I hear from my heart. Another *moment*. Delivered through AC/DC. "For those about to rock — BAM — we sa-lute you!"

That's me! I'm that. I'm about to rock. I have no idea what that means, but that's where I'm going. Screaming headlong into the storm in the middle of the night, I mash down on the accelerator. This night will be my birth — if I survive it. Swerve. And even if I don't. Rumble strip. I have no idea what I'm being born to; just a sense that I want to get away from all that is behind me, all that is outgrown, overstayed, and wrong. I want to be born! I want to be born! I want to be born!

It feels great to challenge death like that, for a while. But for oAC/DC song, there's a Bryan Adams one coming. *There was th*ᵉ *and me, we were wild and young and free* ... I don't care, vay I'm going to die in a high-speed crash in a Kansas tornado in the middle of the night with Bryan Adams singing me into eternity. "Heaven" my butt. So I decide to slog through the rest of the storm at a more reasonable speed, thinking about one core curiosity.

I knew nearly nothing about God when I signed up for a life with him. I was a kid, fourteen years old, when I decided to trust him. I pictured myself hanging from a trapeze on a cloud, and imagined myself letting go. I had no idea what I was getting into. I had only a vague understanding of what sin was. I certainly didn't even begin to understand how some guy dying on a cross could have any impact on me. Prayers were the not-quite rhymes we said before dinner, or the fluffy stuff pastors in black robes intoned with their hands raised over the congregation before they let us go to lunch. Worship was droning through more not-quite rhymes in the hymnbook and trying to figure out how to sing along with the impossibly high notes of songs clearly written for old ladies with brooches and blue hair. I didn't know a thing about what I was doing when I prayed for God to take control of my life.

All I knew was that I felt something missing. Or I felt something to be gained. Or I knew there was something real being articulated, something of an audacious truth I'd never admit to on my own but was able to respond to with an unexamined sort of shrug. And that's all that was requested of me. Glenn told me that all God needed was a little nod toward the question of "Do you want to give your life to someone who loves it, and you, more than you do?"

I nodded. I needed a friend. I wanted to belong. I was part of a mass of people who needed an opiate. All of the things that are said of Christians by people who belittle the gullibility of Christians were true of me. But it was the one time in my life when I was offered something real, and there was something real, profoundly real, about the thing I encountered and to which I gave my nod. The fact is that

I was not solid, I was not strong, I was not even all that real, but that has no bearing on the existence of the thing to which I was responding. I think the very fact that someone knowing so little, with so many obvious needs, could have such a moment is the best evidence I have that I was interacting with something real. And if God is real, then, well, that changes everything.

Or so I thought. But I was wrong. It turns out that we're already living in God's world — he doesn't offer the welcome package like we get when we first arrive at Disney World. I thought my prayer would change everything, but it didn't. I suppose I was a tiny bit changed right away, mostly just in that I had a different sense of self-description and an absolutely elementary claim to a different life trajectory. But in no way did everything feel changed. I still did the same things I'd ever done, both good and bad. I still couldn't see through walls or tell the future. I couldn't read minds or bend spoons by staring at them. I couldn't make a mountain throw itself into the sea like the Bible said I'd be able to do if I mustered faith the size of a mustard seed. And frankly, I was a bit thrown by this.

I didn't know why things hadn't changed more. I didn't know why I wasn't happier, or why I didn't feel some huge liberation, or why I didn't feel absolutely sure about the reality of the God who'd been real enough for me to give my life to him. But it turns out my problem wasn't that things hadn't changed; my problem was that I didn't know how to tell that they'd changed.

In college I smoked pot a few times. I remember saying, as is stereotypical, that I didn't think it affected me, but then one time I was in the back seat of a friend's car, high, and there was this riff from a John Mellencamp song that came around. *Da-da, da-doop, do-doop.* Wow! I thought, of all the sounds in the world, what are the odds that those three would be put together? I began to ruminate, my mind in awe about what I'd experienced. And then the riff came

around again: *da-da, da-doop, do-doop.* Un-freaking-believable! All
the sounds in the world, and those three were chosen once, and then
a second time! Amazing! Staggering!

And that's the moment I understood that pot did, indeed, affect
me. But it was a different experience than drinking, with no obvious
physical evidence for me to point to. It took a moment of altered
perception for me to see that something had most certainly changed
for me.

I'm having that same feeling as I bounce through Kansas on the
mildewed bench seat of this rattletrap truck. I never would have seen
this coming. Amazing how perceptions change.

Things with God are like that, though, and there are a great
many times when they feel about as rational as being blown away by
the miracle of music. I think they're supposed to feel that way, and it
makes sense that they would. If God created everything, that would
include the ordinary world — the mundane, corporeal stuff to which
firm rules and understandings apply. But creation would also have
to include all of the stuff that doesn't fit neatly into our eighteen or
so hard-and-fast rules about the world. Things like love, forgiveness,
peace, endurance, sacrifice, obedience, submission, conviction, sin,
holiness, authority, salvation, damnation, time, eternity, heaven, hell,
souls, union, hope, grace, moments with Russ Taff or AC/DC — all
of this needs more than what the rational world can make sense
of. And it all sounds a lot like some stoned Hoosier in the back of
a Caprice Classic listening to John Mellencamp on the way to Big
Red Liquors. That's just the way it is, and you don't know you've
slipped the bonds of the very small rational world until the moment
when some bit of eternity tackles you, blows your mind, and refuses
to travel with you back into the world where God's ways seem more
than a little bit weird.

And in the moments where you're tackled and your mind is blown, you have no doubt that what you're experiencing is worth the cost of being a weirdo. You have no doubt that what you're experiencing is the truth about the world, and that the truth goes beyond what's shown on the six o'clock news or taught in textbooks. Being weird is absolutely preferable to the alternative of staying in the smaller world. It's worth trying to make some changes to the collection of protective self-definition piled on your crab shell. It makes you think about the silliness of a life preserved by hiding with no hope of ever revealing your true self.

But when the prayer is over and you open your eyes back to the sober world, the narrow world, the world of bills to pay and firm rules for civil society, man, you'd pretty much have to be stoned to risk coming out of hiding for real.

I want to try it, though. I want to live like a stoned Hoosier. I'm on my way to Denver to start a new life, because over the course of several months there was a needling sense of invitation to More.

I've been asked to move, and I feel a desire to take God at his word and see what happens. I want to share some living experience of him with other people. Of course, I want those experiences to happen in a context with which I'm familiar, but I know that the context is my filter, not the truth, and that I'm going to have to get comfortable with responding to invitations that don't always make sense to me. I guess that would be my goal while I'm in Denver: to learn to recognize and respond to invitations not because they make sense, but because of who's offering them and because I believe that the best I can do with most of life is to nod in response to the greater reality when it asks if I want to come along. And if I survive the tornados and the storms tonight, maybe I'll change the world.

PART II

THE LURE OF HEROES

CHAPTER 8

The Deal About Scaffolds

"Your problem isn't that you're gay. It's that you're a jerk."

This is my version of tough-love truth and renegade honesty. Sitting across from me in the beautifully decorated living room of his 1920s bungalow, on the chaise before the fireplace, is my landlord and roommate, Stephen. I've been in Denver for almost six months and am finishing up my first quarter of seminary. It's already clear to me that the biggest problem regarding the continuation of sin in the world is the way we tiptoe around it and let ourselves be defined by our favorite-flavored spiritual maladies. We hide behind our shortcomings, sins, and failures just as readily as we hide behind any of the other externals we apply to our crab shells as camouflage from the squids — because sometimes we can't tell the difference between being seen by benevolent eyes and being seen through the eyes of a predator. All we know is that we want to be invisible. We take that camouflage and fashion idols from it — trinkets that offer us evidence or excuse about our importance or lack of it, and evidence or excuse about why we should be loved, or loved because our flaws are not our fault and should not be held against us. Stephen's problem isn't that he's gay — it's that he's a jerk.

"What does that even mean?" Stephen is in his midthirties but is still in good shape and very fashionable. He tends to be somewhat bitter, and it drives me nuts that he can't just submit to truth in his life. He's alternated between fighting against and rolling with the gay life since college, when he first named his desires. It wasn't exactly the popular thing to discover about oneself as a leader at his small Christian school. He believes it's nurture, not nature, and he believes his homosexual behavior is sinful. He's been in counseling about it for some time, but he also has a boyfriend. The boyfriend, to his credit, is really a great guy, and if homosexuality were kosher they'd make a wonderful couple.

"I don't think your struggles with homosexuality are the real problem. I think of sin like a well that narrows as we go deeper into it, and as we fall, we carry these boards with us, these things we call sin, and we only fall until the board jams into the sides of the well. Those boards make the scaffolding of the sin we're willing to admit. We stand on a board and we say, 'This is my worst sin — there is nothing darker than this about me,' and we swear that the board we're on is not a board, is not a scaffold, but is really the bottom of the well. You think your gay tendencies are the worst thing about you, that they're what force you to the bottom of your well. You seem to think that if you could clear up that struggle, you'd be okay — or at least you'd be able to work your way up out of the well by cleaning up other things."

He takes a sip of his margarita, looking at me dubiously as I continue.

"But the truth is that if you could remove that board, the board of your gay junk, you'd find yourself falling downward because there are still many things that are darker and more odious about you than that particular issue. Your problem is not that you're gay. Your problem is that you're a jerk because you think your gayness is the furthest extent of your problem."

"Do I? Is that your incredible diagnosis? Should I just go change that real quick?"

I realize that I'm making the face I'd make with Betsy if she got upset over an honest reply about a new haircut. "I'm not trying to make you angry, Stephen. I'm not trying to hurt your feelings. I'm just saying this because I see you hurting and fixating on something that's a worthy struggle, but it's not more important than you are. And the more obsessed you become with fighting it, the harder it will be to let go of, and the less aware you'll be of the other areas of your life that could use a little attention and where some success could do you good."

"So maybe I'm defining myself too much by my sin?"

"Exactly."

"Hmm. So, when you go to church and they ask for prayer requests, what are your requests?"

"I don't want to get into a fight, Stephen. This isn't about me."

Stephen grins. "Okay, try this one. This morning I stood in a circle holding hands with the other people from the praise band, doing prayer requests. The pastor's wife asked for prayer for her kids. She said they have such rebellious spirits. The kids are two and three years old!"

I laugh.

"I'm not making this up! Being the pastor's wife, she's pretty guarded, I'll admit. But the next person asked for prayer about the minivan he and his wife are thinking about buying. He said they wanted to honor God with their choice." He raises his eyebrows for emphasis. "Honor God with a minivan choice? Come on! Is this really the pressing issue in his life — the one that's so overwhelming he needs to call in prayer reinforcements?"

"It's pretty dangerous ground to critique other people's prayers very closely, Stephen."

"Would you have shared your prayer requests with them? Would you have risked talking about not being sure about what you're doing with your life? Or being a month late paying me your rent?"

"Probably not," I answer. "But maybe. I don't know. I might have. Yeah, sure. Why not?"

"Here's my prayer request: I went to counseling Friday after work and prayed for freedom from my sins there. Again. For like the millionth time. I cried myself to sleep that night, half-drunk. I took a walk with Corey yesterday and told him that I couldn't see him anymore because I believed that what we're doing is wrong. Which means that I must think he was wrong when he made the choice to leave his wife and kids, and so is the hope he's had for his future with me. I came home, got drunk, and spent the evening alone with my stash of porn, feeling like I'm the only person in the world actually still fighting this battle — everyone in the gay community thinks it's leftover garbage from a repressed society of mutilators. The closest I came to telling anyone at church about it was when someone noticed I was chewing a piece of gum — which you're not supposed to do onstage, but I was chewing it to cover up my alcohol breath — and she asked if I had an extra piece and winked at our shared wickedness when I gave her one." He's angry and red-eyed. "What do they teach you in seminary about sharing my kind of prayer request? Would you share that one? I'd be kicked off the praise team immediately because my sin disqualifies me from worshiping God. Rebellious toddlers and minivan selection — those things are good to take to God and are clean enough to keep a microphone in your hand — but I'd lose the one thread of connection I still feel to this deaf God who won't answer my prayers! My gay issues may not be my definition, and they may not be the bottom of my sin, but you can go to hell if you think I want to go deeper, or if you think it's something that I can carry with me into church as a matter of fact. I know what it would cost me. Look at what it already costs me!"

CHAPTER 9

SALESPEOPLE AND WITNESSES

So that's my roommate, Stephen. We live in the artsy part of town in a three-bedroom place, and we have God talks pretty often. I'm the third seminary student in a row to live with him. His deal is that he can't choose between his idol and his God, so he keeps both of them torturously close to him. It's not unlike me and Betsy in some ways — it's been six months and we still talk pretty regularly. I pray for her to be stirred by God, for her to see the error in her ways and to choose me. I feel like it's supposed to be finished with her, but I can't give up on her. It's absolutely leftover nice-guy lot. I'm trying hard to let go of her and substitute God stuff in her place, but it hasn't been easy. It's hard to replace an idol you can control, even if it's failing, with a God who doesn't take orders and who loves you but reserves the worship for himself.

Habitat never responded to me, and I can't get past the sweater vests and calling each other "brother" that's everywhere with men's ministries, so I've let that idea go. I've spent this quarter at seminary because David was doing it, and it seemed like it would be a good thing to have some extra letters after my name no matter what I did. I moved out here with cash in the bank, but after buying what has turned out to be a less than serviceable Jeep, paying seminary tuition, and not making any changes to the way I live, things have gotten very tight.

I haven't known what sort of career I'd be interested in, so I've been looking for plain old jobs — something I can do to make some cash while I'm in school. I left an application at 7-Eleven and never got a call back. Boston Market called me in to take a personality test, and then they didn't call back. That felt like bottom. Really, how low do you have to score on a personality test not to be Boston Market material?

It doesn't look like I'm going to end up back in seminary next quarter. I don't want to take out student loans and then try to do ministry with big debts over my head. Glenn said he thought Zionsville Presbyterian would be willing to pay, but by the time they wrote to make it official, I'd already run out of time to enroll — and had decided I didn't really want to go back anyway. I felt a little slighted by their delay, but I know that's just because it shows me that I'm not as important as I want to be. I'm trying to work on that.

Seminary is a lousy place for Christians. At least in the short term. If you're someone who's really strong about what you believe, seminary will unravel that for you. The fact is that there really aren't many, or maybe any, airtight arguments to make about God. There is enough to justify faith, but there is certainly not enough to eliminate doubt or make disbelief an untenable conclusion. For people who come in not knowing this, seminary can be crushing and can take away that sort of faith. I was fortunate in that I didn't know any complicated arguments and didn't have much of a firm stand regarding the basis for my faith, so when I was told that there were no airtight arguments, I sort of shrugged and said, "Okay."

I've learned something else in seminary: the only thing more wimpy and tragic than a pastor is a theology professor. Take all of the nerdiness and uncoolness of a pastor, cram that into a wrinkled corduroy blazer with elbow patches, knot a full Windsor in a 1950s tie, smudge up some thick plastic glasses, and then remove the ability to shave a moustache evenly, and you've got a Denver Seminary professor. That said, the only people I've ever met who live more seriously submitted to God than Glenn are those same professors. Not auspicious in terms of making a person want to convert, but I suppose that's another example of where the arguments aren't airtight: is living like those people worth how it'll make me look? Am I willing to trade the praise of cool people for the praise of church people, whose praise, while uncool and available to uncool people, is tied to something that feels bigger?

Seminary is also bad for people like me, people who see additional schooling as a hoop to jump through on the way to actually doing something with their faith. I can't think of a single practical course available there. Even the Hebrew won't help — it's outdated the way Shakespearean English is outdated. Seminary offers tools, and that's good, I guess; it keeps people telling a more consistent story. But the actual content a person learns in seminary is all presented as though it will amount to a grand airtight argument, even though we've already decided such a thing doesn't exist. So what it comes down to, instead, is an education that leaves seminarians knowing how to go a few steps further in their arguments than the people with whom they argue, but they still can't ever close the deal with an argument. People simply don't work that way.

I think the real question Christians need to ask is whether they're called to be salespeople or witnesses. A salesperson knows the features and benefits matrix and can show you the chart where the "Heaven" column is checked in Christianity but not Judaism, or where "Eternal Individual Existence" shows up for Baptists but not Buddhists. A salesperson enters every interaction looking, by definition, to sell something. They stand for something outside of themselves, some product they want other people to want. But the problem is that the salesperson selling Christianity can't ever sell the faith by working from the chart alone. Like people who sell cars for a living, Christian salespeople rely on the new car smell, or on how a new convert will look driving Jesus (complete with a little silver fish on their bumper). The sale only comes when the salesperson can answer one question more than the consumer is willing to ask, or when the consumer gives in to a desire to buy for some reason beyond pure empiricism. A successful salesperson, the one with their name on the plaque on the wall, knows this and finds a way to manage the frustration that comes from selling without being able to make an airtight case. Usually that coping technique is a deadening, Machiavellian cynicism that is only able to sell an external faith. And a merely external faith is the deadliest thing in the world — it's just another idol — and there are corpses all over the place to prove it.

Something within us knows we're meant for better than the lie we create when we present ourselves as salespeople for a God we can't sell in truly meaningful ways. The role of salesperson doesn't fit us properly, but rather than admitting this, we look for new heroes and redouble our efforts to polish our pitch.

The other option is to be a witness. Witnesses don't have to explain what they've experienced, at least not beyond the best of their understanding. Their only burden is to speak of what they've experienced of God in their ordinary lives. Like a salesperson, a witness will speak of something beyond the witness, namely God. But a witness represents only the witness, and the exchange between believer and unbeliever is just an exchange between two people, not an exchange between hunted and sensitive-voiced hunter. With witnesses, both people remain people, created, contingent, and courteous. And God remains God, able to show up however God wants to show up, free of the narrow descriptions upon which a salesperson builds carnivorous promises. The Bible is full of talk about witnesses. Seminaries are full of salespeople in training.

There's a place for both, of course. It's a foolish thing to expect that the God who created everything would need us to stand in a single-file line. What I find frustrating, and what has me planning to do something else after this quarter, is that by definition salespeople will tend to build arguments to prove that their way is the best or only way. There's a comfort in having answers. It's an angry, bitter, fearful sort of comfort, but it has a tremendous gravity for timid souls like mine who want to hide. I would love to bury myself in answers. I would gladly choose hiding over heaven, idols before God, respect instead of repentance. It's hard to be near seminary's sort of gravity without getting sucked in by it. I'm glad that circumstances have worked out that I'm leaving sales school, but I know that if circumstances had allowed me to stay, I'd be gathering answers as camouflage for my crab shell as greedily as anyone there.

We're called to be servants to everyone, and there is work for me to do in the world. Mostly that consists of pointing out the reality of God in ordinary life. I'm excited about my role in that. It answers questions with questions: Who am I? Well, who would God have me be? It's an answer, but it's fluid. I dig that. I get to feel important and loved, but I get to feel it in the form of God's smile.

CHAPTER 10

Rachel Likes Me

Betsy and I still talk maybe once a week; there are a lot of questions and leftover emotions for both of us. Lingering bad habits, mostly. It turns out she's seeing two guys — the guy she was seeing behind my back, and another guy she's seeing behind his. I have to think that means her choices had more to do with her than they had to do with me, and that makes me feel better. I feel stupid talking to her, and I know it's weak comfort I pay a huge price to experience, but I guess bad habits are just like that. She says I should be looking for someone new, and I'm trying. I need to find a better, healthier way to invest the love I have to give.

There is one prospect at seminary. A nice girl, fun and smart and passionate about her faith. Rachel is strong and stunningly beautiful. She has serious opinions about things. She sings and she hugs a lot. A force of nature, some would call her. All the guys on the small seminary campus know exactly who she is because of her beauty, but on a Baptist campus her larger-than-life personality and affectionate tendencies attract as much scorn as pursuit. I know there are several guys who are interested in her. I might be one of them, but it seems like such a long shot that I've assumed I must be misreading her. Then the other day she let it slip that she'd told one of her friends that I was *the one*. She obviously didn't mean to tell me that, and when she immediately hurried to change the topic, I let her.

I don't know what I think. She seems like a good idea in many ways. We have overlapping beliefs and passions. We have similar levels of openness to our personalities and to the choices we make in life. It would be easy enough to just go with it — to shrug and let her lead me away to whatever house and life she has picked out. I think a whole lot of people do that, with relationships and with a lot of other things in life, and I can see the appeal. It's like the report cards have been handed out, and I've passed. No more worrying, nothing left to accomplish. And sometimes a passing grade in a course you don't care much about sounds pretty good when you compare it to a strong chance of failure in a class you're not sure you can handle.

Rachel's father left the family when she was young, and there are times where her need for male validation is obvious — times where I know my nice guy tendency really draws her to me. In some ways she's a lot like Betsy, but there is one huge difference: she talks. And talks. And talks. But it's refreshing because I've spent years playing both parts in my romantic relationships, and it feels good to be pursued. She calls me. She leaves cute messages. She's a mother bear about her mother and younger brother, and she would be about me if I'd let her. She says she's a bit of an altar hound, which means that she likes to cry at church and go down front to have people pray for her a lot. It means that she's emotionally open. She comes from a charismatic tradition and has lots of scars about men and women, about leadership and submission and truth and worth and all of that. She always wants to pray on the phone. I hate that. I still don't like praying out loud, especially with other people, but especially on the phone, and especially, *especially* as the tidy summation of a flirty conversation.

Rachel makes me wonder if I was like her with Betsy or the girl from the other high school. I know I must have been, but it sure feels gross to think so. I don't want someone who says they know me so well or who gives herself to me so readily that there's nothing left for me to pine for.

I need the pining. I don't like easy compliments. I know people say it's bad to choose someone for how they'll make you look, but I think maybe that's just something people say to look good themselves. Don't we all tend to gravitate to people a little up from us on whatever scale we care about? Beauty, brains, fame, fortune, wisdom, experience, whatever? Don't we all tend to get our personal bearings at least in part by the people we attach ourselves to? Isn't that why in high school it's cooler to date a senior than a sophomore? Isn't exclusivity what makes hot restaurants or clubs hot in the first place? Isn't that what sells movies and magazines? Everyone wants to be part of a "cute couple" — that's part of what makes calling a couple cute such a safe compliment. I think we all have this thing inside of us that takes wherever we're at and looks to upgrade. That's what makes the world go around. Ask Betsy.

Until we figure out just how high on the social food chain we can hunt, and then make our final choices, we want something to pine for. We want to fixate on something slightly unattainable, something that will make us feel important for earning its approval and its love. Our aspirations define us, don't they?

It freaks me out that Rachel seems so attainable. She's way out of my league, and there's something about the way she offers herself that makes me not quite trust her. I want to be the one to pursue her. I want to be a hunter, not a farmer.

Not an especially noble little character defect in me, I guess.

CHAPTER 11

WAITING FOR AIR FORCE ONE

I keep thinking about the fact that if I die, I will go to heaven, but so long as I'm alive I'll know the pain of life. My credit cards are taut with burden. Betsy and I haven't spoken for a few weeks. Rachel is high pressure, but in a coy and tedious way. She's trying to get me to make the first move, to her specifications, and that's annoying. I still don't know about her, and I'm still feeling gun shy about women in general. I can't help thinking she'd lose interest in me soon enough anyway. I was relieved to get away from some of that drama when the quarter ended and I didn't have to be on campus every day. I've been doing mostly volunteer church stuff for the past couple of weeks. I don't know where I'm heading. In a phone call home the other day, my mother mentioned that she misses being able to brag about me.

That one stung.

Being alive is disorienting, disappointing, frustrating, humiliating, and just generally hard. I've given up hope that anything I assumed I'd experience here will actually happen; it's clear to me that

I'm destined for something much closer to the rat hole in Calcutta than I'd expected, and I don't know what good I'm doing anyway. It's been nearly seven months since I left Chicago, and I feel lost and broken and like an absolute fool, with nothing to make sense of the choices I've made. I have almost no friends — just David, Rachel and the confusion she brings, a couple of acquaintances from school, Stephen, and the youth group David leads. I have no job, no plan, and it sure feels as though I have no control over what's next. My dad is concerned about my mental health, but then again everyone who works at Lilly thinks the world needs Prozac. I've lived my whole life in a bubble of life assumptions endowed to me by a culture of selfish consumption. I have no idea who I am apart from that, and I'm completely unprepared to be here, alone and making choices without the herd. It's confusing and it's frightening — even as it feeds my pride to be on this "rebel for God" track. I'm miserable. I don't know what God wants to do with me and with my life, how he'll make this all work out, and I don't know how to fill in the blanks on my own. I can say all of this casually, but it tweaks the deepest parts of me to feel like I'm derailed. The feelings make me desperate to take control, so at night sometimes I put on my cross necklace and go to the roughest parts of town hoping to get shot. Suicide by carefully chosen wrong place at wrong time. Heaven without passing "Go." On my terms.

Tonight I only made it a few blocks, to the corner of Colfax and Josephine, in front of the 7-Eleven that never responded to my application. I was planning to drive to an area near Five Points, where the risks are greater, but I saw this one-legged black guy in an Army jacket in the bus shelter, and I stopped.

His name is George, and he's more than a little drunk. His left pant leg is folded over and pinned at the nub where his knee used to be. He dropped his metal crutches on the ground at his foot. He wet himself and smells like it, plus sweat and alcohol. It's cold enough that I wonder if his pants will freeze. He tells me that Air Force One is waiting for him out at the airport, and he wants me to take him there. I ask about his world, but he is so far gone that he can't report on anything but his immediate surroundings. I ask him if he's hungry, and he is. I buy him a ham and cheese sandwich from the 7-Eleven cooler. He doesn't have any teeth, so he can't bite through the ham. I'd noticed his missing teeth — I should have thought to select a different sandwich. What he can bite off, the bread and cheese, he gums without swallowing. He fishes a hooked finger across the roof of his mouth and flings each bite to the ground, and then wipes his hand on his wet pants. Clearly, his drinking has reached the point that he's given up food for booze. His coughing makes me think of the news report I heard today about a tuberculosis outbreak that has the firefighters and paramedics concerned about the people they pick up.

I try to make conversation with him for an hour, with little progress. He's still far from sober, but his stupor is clearing, and he asks about me. I tell him about seminary and moving from Chicago. I tell him about Betsy and Rachel.

"Laaadies," he blurts in slur. Then, in whimsical free association follow-up, "I loves me some ladies."

I tell him about how I go out at night with weird thoughts of getting killed and escaping the pain.

"I hear that. Air Force One's going down one day, and that'll be that," he empathizes.

For a long time we just sit on the bench, him taking and scraping bites of cheese sandwich from the roof of his mouth. He puts the ham in his coat pocket.

I don't know why I'm sitting here with this guy. I don't know what I can do for him. Frankly, it seems pretty clear that he's not long for the world. I ask him if he'd like to pray with me. He offers me his hand. My hands have been pulled into my sleeves to minimize my exposure to his coughing and fluids. My first thought is to recoil, to protect myself. But my first action is to push my hand out from my sleeve and take hold of his, which happens to be the one he favors for fishing bites from his mouth. I pray and he coughs and shudders. I say Amen. He says Amen.

And he doesn't let go of my hand.

So I don't either.

And we sit that way for about another hour, fat white do-gooder and one-legged wino near the end of his tour, holding hands in the bus stop on Denver's main drag for sin and vice. I don't know which of us is more desperate, and I don't know which of us is more buoyed by this time. I think briefly of those stories where people meet someone who they think may have turned out to be an angel. There's something nice about the idea of a repulsive, sodden angel holding my hand, especially since I left home hoping to get shot.

This is better.

This is what God had in mind instead of shaping culture with the power of mass marketing like Ivy would have had me do. This is what was more important than my dreams with Betsy. It's what was more pressing than my parents' plans for my life. George. He is evidence of a stoned Hoosier reality. He is more important because if I hadn't shown up he'd have spent the night alone and forgotten. So would I. The world is full of people like us and moments like this, and they make sense of all the questions that can never be answered by seminarians and people who live in ivory towers of rationalizations and convenience. My mom would be horrified and could never brag about such things to her friends over coffee, but my heavenly Father is proud. This moment has nothing to do with my hiding places — my defense and camouflage. The collection I affix to my crab shell to protect myself from the squid of life and evil has nothing to do with this moment. I'm here. I'm seen. I'm exposed, and

God is with me. This makes sense of my situation. This makes me worth something. I'm important and I'm loved, and all the worship remains with God.

About an hour before sunrise, I put newspaper down on my Jeep's passenger seat and drive George to a drunk tank he tells me about. I go home and sleep for a few hours. When I return to the place to offer him breakfast, he's already gone. I conclude that if I get tuberculosis, it was worth it, and I get my wish to escape the pain that returns with the ordinary day.

CHAPTER 12

A Load of Sunshine

My Jeep died around the corner from the house last week. There had already been problems with it. Among other things, there is silicon floating loose in the radiator, which I'm told is not a particularly good thing. It also won't pass emissions, so I won't be able to renew the plates anyway. I don't have the money to fix it. I don't even have the money to move it, or to pay the ticket I found on the windshield. Someone broke a window to steal the radio and tapes from it — though they left the Christian stuff. You know Christian music is bad when thieves who are in enough of a rush that they'll break a window take time to reject some of the tapes they find inside. I visited the scene of the crime to duct tape some cardboard into the hole where the window was and then slogged home along the uneven sidewalks trying not to break my neck in what I hope is the last snow of spring.

My world feels about like that on all fronts. Broken down, broke, and stranded, with what remains inside proving absurd and unwanted even by desperate people. And outside all is treacherous and inhospitable. All that felt so exciting, so promising, so worth risking for when I moved here, has turned out to be a lemon. When I call home, I still talk about how beautiful the scenery is here and how the weather is better, and I still have experiences with God that I try to shape into stories to placate my mother's fear for my safety and my sanity; but most of my energy seems to go into simply coping. And my mom misses being able to brag about me.

I'm sure she didn't mean it like *that*, but come on.

If I could admit it without absolutely breaking down or feeling completely lost, I'd say this has been a mistake. But I can't say that. I can't admit that. At least not yet. There has to be something worth experiencing beyond life as a Christian hobbyist. I want to get into the dirt and doubt of the real world. It hurts, but all I can do is push forward.

I talk to Rachel a lot, but never about feeling dissatisfied; that would sound too much like a lack of faith. We talk about my Bible studies or moments with homeless guys or about faith in the workplace or about her participation in Denver's war on pornography. She uses terms like "tremendous man of God" to describe different leaders in her church's world. My impression is that people who are doing "mighty things for the Lord" tend to be real jerks, with a singularity of meritorious focus that justifies them in the eyes of the masses who, in turn, are kept always at arm's length, too far from the details of their heroes' lives to see what's really going on.

But there's something about the culture that I've begun to find attractive.

I want to feel important. I want to feel as though there's a good reason to love me, and God's a pretty good reason. I want to make progress with him. I want to know him, and I want to know his pleasure. I want him to be proud of me. I want people to like him because of me. And yes, I want people to like me because of him. It would be cool to be beautiful because of the God stuff with which I was associated. It would be cool to be a holy man. Maybe not a public hero, but maybe a quiet hero someone else talks about. I heard about an old man in Boulder who is retired from his job but who donates his time to meet one-on-one for an hour each week with forty college students. It's said that he loves so well that any time one of these forty students expresses even a bit of self-doubt or self-condemnation, the old man cries for them. He sees them the way God sees them. He sees their beauty and their promise, their pain and the truth that lives beneath the pain. He is a simple man, out of the public eye (though I heard about him in a stadium full of people). He quietly loves forty college students, and that is his full-time work. That seems pretty cool. That seems like something I'd expect a holy man to do. That seems like something I'd like to do. I could see that man being a sort of hero for me — as he is already a sort of role model. Does that make him a "tremendous man of God"?

Though for now I'd only be able to experience being a tremendous man of God whose Jeep doesn't work and whose music has been pillaged by discerning thieves. Hooray, me.

What sort of hero am I? Maybe you'd care to have me regale you with some of my new thoughts about Pascal and how man is but a worm? I could be that sort of genius. Would you care for a ham and cheese sandwich and some quality time at a bus stop in the middle of the night? I can be that kind of charitable. Maybe you could say something negative about yourself and let me cry for you? I can be that kind of nice guy. Or, better yet, perhaps I could interest you in some used Christian music tapes? How'd that be for a tremendous man of God?

CHAPTER 13

A Change of Scenery

It's June, and I'm sitting on the hip roof of a bright red barn surrounded by the scrubby buttes, alkali gulches, and jagged green mountains of the Colorado–Utah border — where a bunch of John Wayne movies were filmed — watching a canary yellow crop duster cut through the blue sky, popping in and out of view as it dusts the fields of lettuce and Olathe sweet corn. The colors and the sunshine and the fact that there's nothing else I'm supposed to be doing right now make me happy. I don't notice being happy often enough. I like being happy. Hey, thanks God.

Behind me is the window into the apartment I've been calling home for the past three weeks — one bedroom, a small kitchen, a tiny bathroom, and a space for a chair and my radio. The room comes with the job. The rest of the giant barn-turned-church-turned-residential-treatment facility belongs to the good men of Turnaround, a drug and alcohol and whatever-else-you've-got rehab program. It's a yearlong program built around discipline and Bible study and church attendance and physical labor to pay the program's bills. I'm part teacher, part cook, part counselor, part driver, part prayer warrior, and part low-level staff. Most of the time I feel like the guard with the mirrored sunglasses in *Cool Hand Luke*. I'm the morning shift; another person with a similar job description takes over in the afternoon.

The job includes getting up at five o'clock; starting breakfast for the ten men in the program; waking the men up at six o'clock; making sure they're bathed, fed, prayed with, and in class by eight-thirty; grading their work; preparing lunch; dropping most of them off wherever they're working that day; running the donated expired food that goes too bad for our use out to a nearby farmer's pigs; and venturing into town to pick up replacement expired groceries from the Piggly Wiggly. On Wednesday evenings, or Sunday both mornings and evenings, my job also includes driving the guys to church — either the Pentecostal place in town, which is small and friendly, or the one ten miles north, in what feels like the big city compared to everything else along the western slope.

Other Turnaround employees include a couple who are administrators and something like house parents, an executive director who does a lot of fundraising around the state, and Norb, the white-haired gentle spirit who takes meticulous care of everything — down to having special carpet on the dashboard of his Toyota Corolla to protect it from the sun. Norb's primary role seems to be to pray for the men and to be around for them after they leave the program. The fundraiser doesn't live on site, but the rest of us do. It's hot and dusty and there's no air-conditioning; but it's a dry heat, as they say, and it's been fun living in a setting that feels like a country music video.

Rachel was thrilled that I'd taken the job — she knew about Turnaround and believed they were doing "tremendous things for the Lord." I liked that she was impressed. I could understand why the choice to take the job made her like me more. That made me feel important. I found out about Turnaround in the newspaper classifieds and was hired on the spot. The way it works is that I stay here for three months and then decide whether I want to commit for the rest of a year. They say staff consistency is critical to the program's success, so they do the tryout and then ask for the commitment. My pay is three hundred dollars a month, plus the room and my share of the donated expired food. They pay at the end of every month, so for June all I'm getting is the room and food.

Most of my stuff is still at Stephen's house, in his basement in case he decides to rent my room to someone else. I was able to get the Jeep to start and stay running long enough to get it to a dealership described by one of its own salesmen as "the bottom of the barrel." I paid three thousand for the heap in October, and because I knew what it was supposed to cost to repair, and because I'd read something from an early Christian monk about making sure to lose just a little in every financial exchange so you never take advantage of the other guy, when the salesman asked how much I wanted for the Jeep, I told him six hundred dollars. He wrote me a check immediately, and later in the transaction said he'd be able to sell the thing for a thousand dollars the next day. I felt a little foolish, but at least I was able to pay Stephen the rent I owed him, and my credit card minimums too. With Turnaround not paying me this month, I'll miss a month with the credit cards, so in July my entire check will go to the minimums and the late fees I'll incur. I keep thinking about my dad's line of, "Losses are a part of life, but you can't make them up in volume." Turnaround is not his idea of a good idea. My financial situation makes the gulf between us that much wider, and growing.

But the work here matters, and that makes me feel like I do too. The men are here because their addictions have defeated them. Judges have given them the choice of this or prison, or wives have made them choose between this and divorce, or parents have said it's either Turnaround or the streets. The men arrive absolutely tied to their sin, both in terms of how they go about their average day and in terms of how they view themselves. They have become their addictions. The camouflage that was once simple fun or acceptance from friends has gone virulent and consumed the rest of these guys' feelings of identity or protection and has begun to eat through the shell. They smell of rot, and the squids search them out. These men are at the ends of their ropes, unable to distinguish between who they really are and what they've been doing, and they are desperate to glimpse a bit of hope running contrary to the expectations left them by their addictions. What I say to them, and how I treat them, and whether or not I spend time praying for them — to impact them and to prepare myself to be with them — matter. Lives hang in the balance, literally.

Other than that, there isn't a lot to do here. I don't have a car, and I can't just borrow the Turnaround van anytime I want it. When I'm not on duty, I either hide, sweating, up in my room, or I play chess with the guys. A person can only play so much chess, though, and the guys have other obligations here, so that leaves plenty of time to sit out on the roof and journal or read or pray.

And all of that time on the roof, plus all the time at church and the time spent observing how serious things are for the guys in the program, combine to make life feel a lot more about God than it can when there are more distractions. I've started praying kneeling beside my bed at night, the box fan cranked up all the way in the window and blowing noisily onto me. I've never been all that much into prayer, and I've certainly never been one to literally kneel beside the bed, but it didn't take long to realize the value of physically submitting myself to God, whether I felt the hocus pocus of it or not. There are conflicts in the lives of the men here every day, and as much as anything I realized that I was going to have to find some way to hand those issues over to God, or else they would eat me up. But there's been a surprise: it feels good to pray.

I had a cool experience because of all this time and prayer last night. I was thinking about how we're supposed to love God and Jesus. But I don't think a person can love God without the help of God. I mean, I'm grateful that I've been born. I'm grateful that God loves me. I'm grateful that I've been forgiven my sins through the atoning work of Jesus on the cross. But love? Not really. I didn't ask to be saved, and for that matter, I think it's a pretty bum deal that I was born into sin in the first place. The whole interaction is pretty coerced, to tell the truth, and Jesus asking to be loved seems a bit much. What are my choices, really? I want what God offers me, and I want to experience a life with the Holy Spirit, but I've never quite been able to get to the point of saying that I love Jesus. People talk about having a "personal relationship with Jesus," which is fine and good, but I've never had a personal relationship — let alone a loving one — with an invisible friend, or a person who wasn't willing to be present with me and communicate in ways that I understand without some sort of scrunch-eyed concentration on my knees in submission. I've felt guilty about not being able to honestly say that I love Jesus — the person, not the concept or the principles or the subculture people seem to mean when they talk about loving him.

Last night something changed. And nothing changed. Mostly, the thought occurred to me that I do, indeed, love the man, the person, Jesus. He is my friend, and I will recognize him when we meet. We will embrace as long-separated brothers, or better, and in that moment I will finally feel the depth of my yearning for him, my missing of him. I sat on my bed and said it aloud.

"I love Jesus."

"I LOVE Jesus."

"I love JEsus."

"Aye luuv JeSUS."

"Se amo Cristo."

And it made me laugh, happily, gratefully, joyfully, finally. It was a stoned Hoosier moment, a moment when an altered perception highlighted that changes were, indeed, taking place within me. It was not something cool about me. It was not a reflection of my efforts. It was not something I was making up. Somewhere, over the course of the past several months, my heart has been changed to a place where I understand previously impossible — even annoying — concepts like loving the God who first condemned me, then saved me, then played coy with me when I was hurting. What I hadn't understood before was that he loved me, and that he was willing to fill me with his love until it was only natural that I would love him too. Isn't that what I was wired to do? It was another moment where I saw that all covenants are God-initiated and God-fulfilled. I love Jesus because God has been changing my heart. I love Jesus with God's love, not my own. That blows my mind — that my heart is shared, indwelled, filled even, by something beyond myself that aches to commune with the larger remainder of itself. Something within me shines through me, transcending my collection of personal descriptors and shell trinkets. Very cool. It makes me want to pray more, to see what else is out there.

CHAPTER 14

When Scaffolding Collapses

When you're a thirty-year-old Cajun grade school dropout pedophile named Critter, and you have been repeatedly interrupted in the bathroom by recovering crack addicts while you're midway through acts of significant personal perversion, you face a bit of a credibility challenge, even if it is your birthday. For the guys in the program, especially for Cajun Critter, recovery is a lonely life, and mercy gets used up quickly, with little extra given for being a good cook or being able play the piano like the best of the old-time tent revivalists. Around here, even a big heart, and a sincere — if sputtering — desire to find freedom from your demons, is difficult to trust. And though everyone argues that sin isn't graded on a curve, grace feels especially stretched when you pray knowing that even among people whose worlds have been ravaged by their addictions, you're the biggest freak in the bunch.

So it wasn't a complete surprise that Critter pulled the stunt he did today. He came to dinner after receiving a birthday phone call from his mother. His eyes were red like he'd been crying, and as he spoke through the crooked teeth that always look like they could fall from his turtle-ish head, he began to choke up.

"My boy died last night." Now he had everyone's attention. Someone asked what happened.

"He was with his mama, and they was on their way back to my mama's house, where he lives, and they got hit by a truck. He died in the helicopter on the way to the doctor's." He started to shake.

Someone immediately suggested we pray with Critter, so we had him sit in a chair and we all stood around him, with hands on his shoulders or his feet or his greasy brown hair, and we prayed for his family, and for him, and that he would not abandon his rehab work at Turnaround. For a few moments Critter wasn't a disgusting pervert; he was a father mourning the loss of his only son, from whom he has already been separated for months.

"Tammy wants me to come on home. She's tore up pretty bad, and she don't want to go through this alone. I'm fixin' to leave, y'all." Which, of course, everyone urged him not to do. Even Rolo, who almost killed Critter this morning for something he saw Critter doing but refuses to talk about.

When the administrator, Dick, called Critter's mother to convey his sympathies and to discuss what Critter should be encouraged to do next, he learned that not only had there been no accident, but also that Critter doesn't even have a child. And Critter's mother has no idea who Tammy might be.

Dick, white-haired Norb, and I call Critter into Dick's office and tell him what we learned. Dick was a rancher for years. He speaks plainly and has given his life to the ministry of Turnaround because he believes in what he sees happen in the men's hearts. It is time for Critter to "come to Jesus," as Dick says.

Critter is defeated. For the longest time he just sits still, gripping the wooden arms of the office chair.

"I don't know why I done it," he finally whispers.

"Son, you're out of slack," Dick says. "I think maybe we've done about all we can do with you."

Norb's eyes dart back and forth between Dick and Critter. He knows what's at stake in the lives here, and he knows how one man bent on self-destruction can drag the rest down. But there are few things as wrenching as dropping a man off at the bus station in town, knowing you're releasing him back into the world that has already nearly destroyed him, and with your throwing in the towel you call him a failure at what seemed like his last chance at redemption. None of us wants to hurry to kick Critter out, angry though we may be. Critter says nothing.

"What do you think?" Dick asks Critter.

"No, sir."

"No sir, what?"

"I don't want to go. I got no place else to go."

"Okay then. We'll give it overnight to pray on it, and we can talk again in the morning."

"Yessir."

"In the meantime, you can't leave the lie hanging out there. You have to make it right with the other men."

At this Critter's face twists in on itself, and he looks like he might vomit. He turns white and his eyes look as though he can't make sense of the pain he feels inside. There is no anger, not the slightest indication that he is going to try to bargain his way out. He knows what he's done, and all I can think about is that in his soul, the scaffolding that he's mistaken for the bottom of the well of his sin is collapsing, and he is shocked to be hurtling down further into the dank, despairing blackness. Bottom is always, always lower than we think it is.

Critter nods. "Can I have a few minutes first?"

"Yeah." Dick answers, returning Critter's file to a desk drawer.

"Would you like me to pray with you?" Norb offers, and Critter begins to sob. Dick and I leave the office.

While Critter and Norb pray, Dick and I gather the other guys and tell them what happened. There is no telling what would happen if Critter broke the news to them himself. It's better to give them a few minutes to digest the news, and then let Critter apologize. Duncan, the other staff person with the job description like my own, except that he's a big-talking graduate of the program himself and about as hard-core military about it all as can be, immediately rises from his chair and leaves the room when Dick says he does not intend to send Critter home.

A nineteen-year-old named Jacob just arrived yesterday, furious with his parents, who tricked him into being here. There are no locks or bars on the place, but it's a very long walk in any direction if a man wants to leave, and Turnaround is a major shock to the system on a normal day. Jacob is visibly freaked out by what he is experiencing. The rumors he's surely heard about Critter already. The story. The prayer. The lie. Duncan's response. And now a public confession. That's quite a first full day in rehab. He is watching it all happening, and he studies the other men when Critter finally enters the room.

Critter already knows what the men think of him. Their opinions are actually probably more generous than what Critter thinks of himself in his more honest moments. But there is something weird about sin, something about the way we battle with it, that makes us somehow embrace the struggle and find something like a glory in it. Among the men at Turnaround there is a real temptation to tell stories about where they've been — war stories — and even to bring some of that battle-based paradigm into the way they relate to one another. Telling stories of darkness is part of the culture when the culture is defined by the sins against which men struggle. There are rules against such storytelling, and we make every effort to shut down those sorts of conversations because all they do is feed the wrong dog in the fight between hope and despair, but they're nearly impossible to eradicate. Serial killers will always have their place in prisons, and people with Critter's issues will always find a parallel niche in rehab facilities — that's just part of how the world looks when people work to earn the praise of their sins. For as much as Critter hates himself for his addictions, and as much as he hates being shunned by the men in the program, there has always been a certain pathetic and soiled security blanket of evil comfort he finds in his position as chief freak.

Today he broke. He was as small a man as I've ever seen, and he let go of his security blanket. It's nearly impossible for me to imagine how terribly frail and insignificant he must have felt. When your last shred of comfort comes from being the guy who is the lowest of the low, and you let even that shred go, you are about as stripped bare as you can be. And then to have to confess and beg forgiveness from a group of men who are already panicked about seeing their own tattered pieces of self-delusory comfort being ripped from them — men to whom you've lied and whose mercy you've already taxed when they prayed for your lie only a short time earlier. How awful. May I never live the moment Critter lived this evening.

"There ain't nothing I can say. I lied to you. I wanted to feel normal for a while on account of my birthday, and I lied to get it. What I done was wrong, and I'm sorry."

The room is silent for so long that I start paying attention to *Forrest Gump*, muted and playing on the television. Nobody makes eye contact with Critter, who stands looking at the carpet in front of him. Finally, Dick breaks the reverie.

"The van's leaving for church in ten minutes. Let's get going."

I don't hear anybody say a word until we are loading into the van, when Jarrod, the insane attacking chess player, says to Critter, "It's your birthday — you should take the front seat." And nobody protests. Maybe Critter got the seat because nobody wanted to have to sit next to him. That would make sense. But I prefer to believe Jarrod demonstrated the right kind of mercy for an addict rebuilding his credibility from zero.

CHAPTER 15

INTERCESSION

It's still the night of Critter's birthday. We went to the tiny double-wide trailer-turned-church in town. Old Sister Iris played an electric guitar laid across her lap, and Norb played the piano. We sang "I'll Fly Away," which has a particular charm in the orange carpeted, flimsy-paneled room with its ten non-Turnaround congregants and their tambourines. Pastor Clarence wished Critter a happy birthday, and the church people clapped for him. By the last song, Critter was singing along. His southern accent — and the fact that he was the only one there who could sing — made him easy to pick out. He was smiling as we climbed back into the van. As we drove home he watched the last shades of red and purple fade over Utah, and a couple of times I saw him close his eyes.

That was earlier. Now I'm on my knees beside my bed, feeling the wind from the fan blow the hair on my back. I think of shaving it. Then I think of my mirror, covered for three days now in dried shaving cream so I won't be able to see my reflection. I'm fasting. I don't know how long I'll go. Maybe forty days. I want God to take my life. My preference would be that it would be taken literally — that I'd die. Same reason as what drove me onto the streets in Denver — I want to escape. And if I don't die, I at least want God to take my life and do something with it. I don't want to be in charge of it anymore — I don't know what to do with it, and I feel like it's not amounting to anything. I'm not satisfied with my collection of personal symbols — my shell's covering isn't making the grade. I want better. I want to be a holy man.

I try to pray. I concentrate. I petition. I think about the day with Critter's breaking, and I pray for his safety among the men during the night. Not that I think anything would actually happen to him, but every morning as I make my way from room to room to wake the men up, I brace myself that someone may be missing, or may be hanging from the ceiling. I try to pray, but I can't get into the groove.

The groove, when I get into it, feels like a conversation, except it isn't built on words. It's more images or whole chunks of satisfying reply — as though God answers not with sentences, not with letters streaming from left to right across my mind's eye, but with paragraphs. And not always with answers to my questions — it's more like he answers the question behind my question. I don't know what it's like for other people, but for me the question behind my question seems to always be something like, "Are you real? Do you see me? Do you love me? Will everything be okay? Daddy?" I know it's pretty far out compared to the world I knew in Chicago — I know how this would sound if I talked about it on MTV — but it's hard to think of a more beautiful thing than when I wait beside my bed, covered in the noise of the fan, and somewhere in the emptiness within me I feel the sweeping answer that wraps me in, "I am. I do. I do. It will. I am. I am. I am."

But tonight I can't get into the groove. When Rachel and I talk on the phone, she likes to pray about angels camping out on the roof of the barn to protect us from demons and such. That image is a bit much for me, but I do know that I can feel a certain disturbance in "the Force" when a man enters or leaves the program. So I pray about Jacob the new guy and for strength for the angels who protect us. Still, I can't click into the groove. So I pray that if God wants me to pray, he'll clear the fog between us. Then I tell him I'll talk to him tomorrow and climb into bed.

A few minutes later I feel him speak, which for me feels like one of my own thoughts, except that I can tell it didn't originate with me — plus it feels benevolent. "Try again now." I return to my knees and feel a real clarity and ache regarding a need I can't identify. The sudden and dramatic change is remarkable, and on a hunch I leave my apartment and head downstairs. I listen outside of Norb's room and hear him praying. I knock.

"Were you just praying for me?" I ask.

"A few minutes ago," he answers, not at all surprised that I'd show up at his door to ask such a question.

"I think maybe I'm supposed to join you — I was blocked and then God said to try again. Is there something in particular going on with you?"

"I'm worried that Shane is relapsing. For the first month after he graduated he was strong and stayed in touch, but he hasn't returned my calls this week, and I'm concerned that he's hiding from me."

"Okay. Do you want to pray together or separately?"

"Stay here, but let's pray on our own for him, and we'll tell each other what we hear."

"Good," I answer, and as I kneel down with my elbows on a chair, I think about how very far I am from where I was a year ago.

I pray differently when I pray for other people. In "tongues." I can tell from the sound and tone, and from something inside of me, what I'm praying in a general way, but it's sort of like the groove-type responses I get from God in that I don't feel like what I'm praying is as narrow-band as words. I'm praying something more communicative somehow. Something more accurate. Something that, frankly, I can't explain. And even though the prayers feel more accurate and more led by God, I have a frustrating tendency to listen to the words and try to figure out what language I'm speaking, because it sounds like a real language. It doesn't take long before I start noticing that there are a lot of Qs, but far fewer Bs in my language than I might have expected. It's nearly impossible for me to pray in tongues without getting overly distracted by the sound of it. So I've learned to quietly sing my prayers rather than speak them. The tune and tone change depending on the person for whom I'm praying, and I can tell a great deal about the prayers based on the song. One time I was praying for a friend's wife and the song turned into something like a Native American dirge chant, and I knew that I was praying for healing for the sexual abuse she'd experienced in high school. That was the first I knew about the abuse, and I cried and cried for her as I sang, as I believe God does. Later, I told my friend about my prayer experience, and he confirmed the things I already knew from the song.

I'm confused by the people on television who pray in tongues in front of huge crowds or the cameras. I have a very strong sense about when it is and is not appropriate to pray in tongues, and in my case it feels like such public displays would be about the most sacrilegious thing I could do. The other thing that seems fairly obvious is that I only get the insights into people's lives that I can handle responsibly. It's not like I get to read someone else's mail, or tell their fortune or something – it's more like I'm able to tell something about the load I'm helping to carry because I can tell what it feels like loaded onto my shoulder. And the secrets I can feel when I help carry a prayer load are as sacred as praying in tongues. I can't imagine a safer confidence than what is shown to someone as they pray for someone else. The only real challenge is that in the light of heaven, all sin is pretty matter-of-fact, and sometimes it can be hard to remember how desperately the person with the sin wants to keep the sin hidden in dark places. That's a horribly foolish strategy, but not as foolish as it would be to break someone's trust by letting the world know what you've been shown in prayer. It's a delicate thing, and I think it's exactly the delicacy of the dynamic that keeps God telling me to keep my big mouth shut. The gift is a lot to handle — at least it has been for me.

I also don't know what to make of the way the gift came to me. After spending the first three years of college convinced that Christianity was nothing more than the cutesy playtime tripe I'd seen so much of, in my senior year I encountered William Blake. He blew my mind, as did the professor who introduced me to Blake. I spent the year on a sort of quest, following from Blake, with his line about "If the doors of perception were cleansed, man would see everything as it is: infinite," to Aldous Huxley's *Doors of Perception*, to Jim Morrison's band The Doors. I read a ton of Native American spirituality stuff. I learned about, and moved away from, the Gnostics. I dove into ancient Chinese philosophy. In fact, it was Chuang Tzu who played the most significant role in pointing me back toward Jesus. He had the system figured out — he had the lock. But he was missing the key. Meanwhile, I'd been walking around with the key tied on a shoestring around my neck, with no real idea what sort of life it was meant to unlock.

The confluence of all those people brought me back to the intellectual conclusion that Jesus was the way, after all. Then a friend from high school called out of the blue to tell me he was getting married and that he'd become a Christian. A loony, raving, Charismatic

Christian whose world was far bigger than he'd ever believed it could be. He caught me on the right day, and over the course of a couple of conversations, I caught the bug too.

I fixated on tongues. It seemed to me that speaking in a prayer language had to be undeniable, unquestionable proof about God. And unlike other gifts, which come and go, I was told the prayer language would be there whenever I chose to pray that way. I concluded that any time I had doubts, I could pray and experience again the undeniable proof of God's reality. I wanted to pray in tongues maybe even more than I wanted to experience God. I begged and pleaded, and for months nothing came.

There's a *Far Side* cartoon where a young man is at the front door to the School for the Gifted, pushing on the door that says, "Pull." That was me with tongues. On the retreat weekend where the gift was given to me, I learned something important about God. He is the pursuer, the initiator. It is my place to ardently desire him, but it is not my place to obsess about what he can do for me. It's part of how he keeps worship for himself — in a good way. When I refuse to see that, he's willing to let me beat myself against walls, or push doors marked "Pull" until I wear myself out. I didn't yet know that the doors of heaven only open outward. Finally, nearly in despair, I relented in my pursuit enough to give God room to open the door; and then he gave me the gift. With it he could have said, "Here — now try to explain *this* to people!"

I can't explain it. And it isn't final and ultimate proof about God any more than the rest of creation already screams of his existence. It won't come with me back through the filters of rationality so I can pin it to a board and dissect it. It's a satisfying gift, and one I'm glad to have been given, but it is no real measure of anyone's position with God, and it doesn't take away the gap I feel between myself and him. And as soon as I got to Chicago after that weekend retreat, I stopped going to church, didn't pray much at all, and spent a year with people who didn't guess I was a Christian. Tongues isn't anything more than one tool, one gift, and there are dozens of others I'm just as good at ignoring.

Tonight, I'm singing quietly into the chair for Shane. Quietly, but ardently; there is a great joy in feeling like you're laboring in prayer — that your efforts are having some sort of real impact someplace else in the physical or spiritual realm.

"I feel like we're supposed to pray for him to wake up," I say.

"So do I," Norb answers.

"Maybe we should call him on the phone," I suggest.

"I don't think that's what God has in mind. Besides, I'm feeling like we're supposed to be praying it — it means something different from what the phone can do."

"Okay," I answer, and for another hour we return to our respective prayers.

I have no solid theological understanding of what tells me that our prayers are finished, and that we've been successful. In fact, it sounds more like Rastafarian "I and I" — meaning "me and the spirit within me" — than Christian doctrine. As I pray, I picture Shane in his bed, asleep. I pray for him to awaken. I sing my prayers. And then I can tell that he is stirring. Not his body — it's still asleep. Not even his conscious self — it's dreaming. What I can tell is that there is a stirring in his spirit. It's more like there was a fire burning in him that he'd let fade to cooling embers, and our prayers have blown them back to a small flame — enough that tomorrow he'll re-engage with his faith. I pray that he will awaken with a worship song in his head, and then I "cool down," amazed at what I've experienced while we've been praying. I thank God for the opportunity as I ask for more of this in the future. I thank him for my being unable to get into the groove before, because if I hadn't been stuck, I may not have noticed when things cleared up, and if I hadn't noticed that, I wouldn't have come to Norb's room.

Norb finishes praying at exactly the same time I do. We hug and say good night.

By the time I get back to my room I'm thinking about how God is making me into a holy man, and thoughts of being a "tremendous man of God" pass through my mind. I know what's going to happen, and I just about have the rationalizations in place for it already. It's my job as junior hero, really. Rachel will be so impressed when I tell her about this in a carefully matter-of-fact way tomorrow. She'll love me more, and she'll know why. And I'll be loved more, and I'll feel important. I'll feel conflicted about it, but tonight was sincere and she played a role in my pursuit of God, so some part of the enjoyment and excitement should be hers too, right? We're just encouraging each other forward, after all.

CHAPTER 16

ALONE IN THE DESERT

It doesn't make any difference how mind-blowing a given experience is, you'll still wake up with drool on the pillow, the same schlub as ever. It's been eight days since Critter's birthday, and yesterday I turned twenty-four. I made birthday phone calls to my parents, and David, and Rachel (who seems to see this time apart as a "refining process" for me, and "us," even though she's been dating a lot recently), and Betsy (who always asks the tacky questions about the men here–details about their deviances and stuff like that, like some sort of long distance sensationalistic daytime talk show) It was the eleventh day of my fast, so there was no birthday dinner.

At least the day was better than it was last year in Chicago.

Sort of. The good news is that during the past year God has claimed me in ways that feel real to me. I have a new sense of identity and purpose, and I know that I'm having a positive impact on people whose worlds are better for my presence in it. The bad news is that I've been left to feed moldy bread to pigs in the middle of nowhere.

Talk about being the prodigal son in the faraway land. And while I know that I'm doing good things, I don't have any idea where all of this is leading. Increasingly, I've begun to wonder if God's response to my offer to give him my life and be a holy man to his glory has been politely declined. Maybe not even all that politely. And at the risk of drawing thunderbolts from God, doing good and being helpful to a few guys out in the boondocks doesn't cut it for me. I mean, the prodigal son probably did just fine eating with and feeding pigs, too, but that option didn't cut it for him so he returned home. I can't express how much I don't want to be like the prodigal son — how much I don't want to have to return home in defeat, even if my dad would come running. I don't want to have been that wrong, or that rejected by God.

The whole way I'm being used frustrates me, but as soon as I start to compile my list of grievances, I remember how I did tell Rachel about my prayer time with Norb, and I did make sure that she was impressed, and I know that just isn't right. When I speak with my mother, I let her be impressed with my abilities to quote chapter and verse from the Bible. I find myself dropping references to seminary with the people I encounter through Turnaround — it impresses them and serves as footnote to the role I play here; a claim to some sort of deferred greatness.

I am a man, and here is an inventory of my desirability credentials: reddish-blond hair and an inability to tan, glasses, three hundred pounds, no car, no cash, no direction, no prospects, no discipline, pride that refuses to submit, partial education (which leaves me opinionated but uninformed), pettiness and a reactionary lust that I keep barely in check by excessive and warping repression, and capping it all, a stubbornness that expresses itself by refusing to step out of the fire that's consuming me.

I pray that it will take me, the fire. That I will die, or that I will live remarkably. I want God to take my life. Take it. Take it. Take it. Admit some value to it by acknowledging it — either end it or redeem it. Stop ignoring me. Stop assigning me to things that are smaller than I want. Yes, I know the inconsistencies are there. I know they include pride. I know they include weakness. I know I'm not God, even to myself. Still I make the demand: take my life — play me or trade me.

Same day, evening. I'm on my way to Grand Junction to pick up my date for the evening. Her name is Sabrina, and she's the fourth cousin of Pastor Clarence from the local Charismatic church, and best friend of Clarence's wife. Sabrina recently returned from a two-year mission term in Israel. I saw her sing at church camp last weekend, and in my gut I had this feeling that she could turn out to be my wife. That would be a good story — two starry-eyed followers of Jesus meet and fall in love as she sings praises, and the young man feels his heart stir. I fell asleep that night memorizing the details of what she wore, what she sang, everything, with every intention of being able to tell friends about it over dinner years into our marriage. After we returned to Turnaround, I told Pastor Clarence about her, and he and his wife helped set up the date. I've been cringing about the card I sent her. The front cover showed a cartoon drawing of a detective holding a rodent in his hand. Inside it read, "My name's Friday. I carry a badger."

Yeah, I'm a catch.

I'm driving an ancient-smelling brown Malibu with a curtain of fabric falling from the ceiling — Dick's emergency vehicle. The engine light is on, and Dick warned me that I might need to pull over to let it cool off some. I have doubts about the car making it all the way to Grand Junction, let alone completing the round trip. A card with directions to the church where Sabrina and I are supposed to meet is on the seat beside me, under the brush and deodorant.

It's been a long time since I wore a button-down shirt or my Polo cologne. I wish I'd made time to get a haircut. I didn't iron the shirt very well, and I can't remember if these are my stinky shoes. I don't suppose it will matter — if she's the one, then she's the one, and if not then none of the other stuff matters anyway.

We meet, and she is lovely. I'd really built her up in my mind, and I was worried that I'd be disappointed, but I'm not. We take her car to Pizza Hut, where she eats a salad, which I read as a lovely aspect of her self-discipline and a reflection of my own new efforts. I drink water with lemon. I tell her about my fast. She tells me about going to church on the Mount of Olives. I ask about her family. She tells me that her father is an engineer. I do my typical joke about, "Oh, really? I love trains." Sabrina's father isn't the sort of engineer that makes the joke work; he actually drives trains. The joke confuses her, and she seems to wonder if I'm making fun of her dad.

We go to the amusement park, where we play miniature golf and take a spin on a couple of the rides. She drives me to the national park just outside of town to watch the sunset from a cliff. She's delightful. She's so nice. She smells good. She's interesting. She's beautiful. I'm so pleased that this is the woman God picked out for me to marry.

We return to the church parking lot. She says she had a good time and thanks me for driving up to see her, and then she practically peals out and disappears into the night. It's obvious that whatever she thought of me, it was less positive than my own conclusions. I drive frantically in the direction where she headed — I want to know if I did something wrong — but I can't find her, and the engine light comes on again, so I grudgingly get out of city traffic and head south back toward home.

What is this? I thought she was going to be the one — I thought God said so. This sucks. I'm embarrassed, and I know Sabrina will tell Clarence's wife about the date and they'll laugh about me together. I'd hung too much hope on meeting my wife. But I want to meet my wife, to get that piece of direction figured out. Once I meet my wife, a huge part of the puzzle will be solved. My life will come into better view. I will have a sort of permanent importance to someone, and nonrefundable love. Instead, I'm left with nothing. Just this borrowed jalopy and a place I don't want to return to in Turnaround. And did I just call that place *home*?

I don't want this life. Why won't God take it? Forget it — I'm not going to wait for him to take it — I'm going to throw it at him. Tears fill my eyes, and the oncoming headlights blur out into stars. I pull off the highway onto a dirt road that disappears into the desert, determined to have one of those dramatic, yelling-at-God scenes like I've seen in movies — like Lieutenant Dan has during the storm at sea in *Forrest Gump*. I tumble from the car, tears streaming down my face, and I suck in a huge breath as I throw my head back to scream for God to take my life.

And then I see the stars.

I didn't know there were so many. And God says to me, in a chunk, "I made the stars. I made everything. And I control the gravities that hold it all together. And I formed your eye and gave you the ability to see what I have made. I am in control, and I have you."

My giant breath comes out in a crippled whisper of surrender, "It's yours."

Then I get back in the car and drive home.

CHAPTER 17

Breaking Fellowship

Turnaround isn't home, and it's time for me to move on. Again. The three-month trial period is just about up, and I have decided not to sign on for the year. David will be here to pick me up in an hour or so. I've struggled with feeling stuck here, and I've disagreed with many of the harsh choices the program makes, but there were two things that happened at church this week that iced the deal for me.

The big church is having a revival, which is something foreign to me. I've always thought of revival as something that happens when God shows up, like Pentecost when he appears as tongues of fire in the room where the disciples are waiting. I've pictured revival being spontaneous. The church has had this event on the calendar for months. There are speakers to book, music to plan, and announcements to produce. People plan their vacations around the revival, and for others the trip to the revival is their vacation. It's probably mostly a semantic thing, when it comes down to it; revival week is really just an invitation to God to reinvigorate people's faith.

Except: There is such a focus on what I've started calling the "holy tickle" that things tend to get screwy. The gifts feel good, and to some people they're pretty impressive. Rachel's whole thing about "tremendous men of God" comes from exactly that impressiveness. And it is impressive to see miracles — for a leg to grow or for demons to be cast out or to have a prophet speak your secrets out loud. The problem is that the gifts are not meant to function like merit badges; they're not intended to create a pecking order. They're not supposed to be the primary focus of the way people interact with God, or with each other. But in some church cultures, that's exactly what they've become, which means people are often tempted to build their whole understanding of God around the recipes they think will produce spiritual abilities in them. Sometimes the desire for the gifts is good, and sometimes it's bad, but there are huge problems that tend to develop when people fall more in love with the voice than they are with the speaker.

"The Jews killed Jesus," the sermon unfolds, "and look what happened to them in World War Two." It's a path of logic that emanates from the desire to figure out how God works and how to work the system to get the holy tickle. It has to do with the magic of innocent blood and the predictability and narrowness of God's justice.

"What did you think of the thing about the Jews?" I ask the Turnaround executive director later. "The part about Hitler as agent of God's justice."

"That's what I've always been taught. Guess I didn't think much about it at all." He finds my questioning to be insubordinate and distasteful.

I don't have an intellectual category to accept the teaching. My understanding of the theology is that Jesus died not because the Jews called for his crucifixion, but because there was no other way for me to be reconciled to God. I could not make up for my sins, and I needed him. The Jews didn't kill Jesus: I did. And in terms of justice for his innocent blood, I guess I see his resurrection, and mine, and the power his blood wields in the world as something like justice. I think the preacher was wrong, whether I'm correct or not, and I think his error comes from an ultimately unwise craving to be a Christian hero. I can't keep his brand of bauble, this iconic flashy hero deal, in my collection. I gouge it from me, along with a piece of myself, I'm sure, and add it to the pile of discarded camouflage, like Betsy or my family or Zionsville or advertising or seminary or whatever else.

And yes, a pile of discarded camouflage can become its own idol, and yes it's growing, fueled by my pride and my fear. And yes, it's just the same as the compliment I've been paying myself my whole life, where I somehow believe that being aware of the game makes me less a victim of it. And yes, maybe that means I haven't made any progress at all. And yes, that freaks me out. But not as much as what happened at the evening service.

There was music and clapping. There was a guest speaker, introduced as "a mighty man of God much blessed by the Lord." He invited people to the front of the church and blew across the mint on his tongue as he touched their foreheads, and they fell to the ground. I sat still. No way. I ducked his eyes. I thought nasty things about him. I did not want to play his game.

He called me up to the front of the church.

Suddenly, I wanted it to be real. He blew across the square spearmint Velamint. I went down. I felt peace. I felt comfort. I felt yellow and just right. I felt laughter, and I felt the Spirit's industrious desire to love me. I felt love — the substance, not the emotion.

After a while, I got up and walked back to my seat. Now I feel embarrassed. I feel angry, even. I don't know what to say about what I experienced. Was it real, or not? I mean, was it really God, or not? Was it just the power of persuasion? Did I just want it to be real? Did

I fall because I wanted this traveling preacher to be holy and great? Tremendous like I've wanted to be tremendous? There was something sweet about the mint — something charming and practical and just . . . I don't know what.

I don't know what to do with it, and I sort of feel duped. Tricked, almost. Like something was taken from me. A part of me feels almost like I did after I lost my virginity — I feel as though I experienced something incredible, but without context or relationship. I can't name it. Maybe it's just my brain getting in the way. I feel ashamed that I was just like all of those people I've always made such fun of on television. Oh, man. What do I do with it? What does it mean? Does the experience mean that everything else about the Pentecostals is also right? Does the stuff where they seem so wrong mean that what I experienced was also wrong?

I can't discard the experience, and I can't attach it to my crab shell either. I can't reject it, but I don't see how it could benefit me or make me more lovable. Something's wrong with my metaphor, with my understandings and appetites and with the way I think the world works.

All I know is that once again I'm amazed that Jesus shows up pretty much anywhere he's invited — often to places where I wish he wouldn't show up. Places I don't approve of. I wish he hadn't shown up. I want him to stay put — right where I left him. But I don't get to decide who Jesus is. And he still seems very happily wed to his bride, the Church, and until he divorces himself from it, I know it would be foolish for me to do so.

That said, the bride's a mess who could use some serious counseling. Ever since Critter's birthday when he lied and then apologized, a real change seems to have come over him. I think his repentance was sincere, and it's possible that some of his temptations were actually removed from him. That's great. Miraculous, even. Glory be to God. But the change has brought him extra attention from Dick and Norb, and from Pastor Clarence too. And that's where the rub comes in. That's where the second reason for leaving Turnaround comes in.

Jarrod, the insane attacking chess player, saw how things were going for Critter. He saw how to earn the praise and extra goodwill of the Turnaround authorities, and he's been asking about what he needs to do to be saved. He also wants to know how he'll know that God has forgiven and saved him. He was told he needed to repent of his sins, which means admitting they were sins and also turning away from them, and he was told he must give his heart to Jesus. He was told that he'd know his prayer worked when the Holy Spirit came into his heart, and he would know this had happened because he would begin to speak in tongues. He was told it usually happens right away.

The evening service rose to a fevered pitch, and an altar call. Most everyone present at the revival already believed, but everyone knew who the Turnaround men were, and several people pointed when Jarrod asked me to go forward with him. I stood behind him as he prayed with the people on the edge of the stage, and then they asked if he wanted to be baptized in the Spirit. One man placed his hands on Jarrod's chest and back. Another anointed Jarrod's forehead with oil. He got the full package from the prayer helper people. And then he started to speak words. The men all exclaimed, "Praise the Lord!" Jarrod looked around at all the celebration that was going on for what he'd let the helpers do for him, and he started hugging them and also saying, "Praise the Lord." I could tell, though, that something wasn't right. Later, I asked about it.

"Did you fake it tonight?"

"Fake what?"

"The tongues thing."

"I don't know. My prayer was real. The other part they just wanted so bad, and the guy was hurting my chest. They said I should open my mouth and let myself start talking. So I did, but nothing came, so I starting talking like they did."

What to say to Jarrod? The guy has nine months left of deconstruction and reconstruction with his life, faith, and sense of self in the program. What to tell him about the imbalance of the churches upon which he's dependent? What to say about my own experiences with prayer, with my own perceptions of appropriateness? How do my own experiences at the revival figure in? And what do I say about the anger and sense of violation I feel now? How to be loyal to Turnaround, and loyal to what I believe to be true from my own experiences? How could I remain a part of this? I decided I could not.

I told Jarrod the Spirit blows where the Spirit blows, and that it always responds to the invitation to enter a man's heart. He had been heard and saved and was loved. The rest would come if that was the Spirit's will. I have no idea what the Turnaround leadership would say about that.

I was angry when I talked to Rachel about the whole thing. I told her what I thought about "tremendous men of God" and the culture that creates them. I told her how painful it was to be associated with the stuff about Hitler and the culture that had introduced Jarrod to what will certainly be a years-long warping experience, if it doesn't turn out to be something that either locks him into a tortured reality or drives him from the faith entirely. I told her I didn't know how I was going to parse through what I'd experienced, how I was going to distinguish between baby and bathwater. I want to serve people — that's what we've been called to do — but there has to be a better way than this. She wanted to pray about it on the phone. I told her I'd talk to her some other time.

PART III

THE COMPANY OF PHILOSOPHERS

CHAPTER 18

ON FILLING CANYONS

It's two weeks later, the last week of August, 1995, and the blue numbers on Jon's car stereo say it's 2:53 in the morning. We're somewhere just outside of Kansas City, heading west on I-70. I've known Jon since about 11:00 yesterday morning, and this is pretty much the first break in our conversation. He looks like a twenty-three-year-old Conan O'Brien, coarse red hair forced grudgingly to obey the part he chisels down the left side of his scalp. He is on his way to Denver to begin his Masters in Philosophy at Denver University. We've spent the time discussing heady God stuff and things like harmonic theory, comparing notes on his understanding of Kant and my understanding of Blake, leapfrogging each other enthusiastically with the next mind-blower. I can tell he'd be a great teacher, and I know I'm a provocative sponge as a student of this sort of thing. It's been a magical drive, and I can already tell we're going to be friends a long time.

But right now we've slipped into a lull, and I think about Rachel, who's driving the car in front of us, who is so beautiful that even the taillights of her Volvo look pretty, and with whom things seem to have recently gotten more complicated; she's mostly given up the idea that we could end up together, or else she's dating aggressively to make a point. Either way, things feel weird, and either way, her backing off makes me miss her and gives room for subtle romantic thoughts to grow in my head.

Last week she called to see if I wanted to ride to Indy with her on her trip home to see family in Cleveland. She and Jon both went to college at Ohio State and know each other from some campus ministry. Jon is from Seven Mile, Ohio, which he describes as "four miles from Three Mile Creek." She looked him up while she was home and learned about his plans, so they decided to caravan west together.

When I first saw Jon, in the parking lot of the Cracker Barrel where Rachel and I had agreed we'd have my mother drop me, I didn't know what to think. David always leaves the door to his apartment on campus open when Rachel comes over — he thinks of her as a sort of temptation, and having her around makes him uncomfortable, but she is pretty and she is fun, and it's not like you can just kick someone like that out, even if you are married. I assumed Jon was what David and I have begun calling Rachel's male friends: the *homme du jour*. The guy of the day.

I'd done the bulk of the driving on the way home, and Rachel spent a lot of time asleep in the back seat. The late hour, my loneliness, and the dutiful role I was playing as driver and protector combined to mess with me. When we'd go under a light I'd look at her in the rearview mirror and say a prayer for her, or an appreciation of the beauty God poured into her. I loved that she bit her nails; it meant that she was down-to-earth. Her hair puddled in chocolate wisps around her cheeks. Her T-shirt rode up to expose a milky white hip as she slept. I drove with my hands at ten and two, to be extra vigilant and extra responsible. Later I told her I thought she was the most beautiful woman I'd ever known. She asked two or three times during the remaining hours of the drive whether I really meant that. I was eager to press home my affirmation of that fact, even though I knew I was on messy nice-guy ground.

Jon laughs. "If you want to know the soul of womanhood in one question, it's, 'Am I pretty'?" He throws his girl voice on the question. "It's straight from the Genesis 3:16 curse where God says Eve's longing will be after her husband. Ever since then female sexual immorality starts and ends with, 'Am I pretty'?"

"But isn't that the role of a man?" I respond. "To build up a woman and make her strong and confident? Especially in a world where the measure of a woman moves ever more shallow with things like beauty and masculine strength or corporate success?"

"Sitting at the feet of a woman and telling her how pretty she is makes her stronger the way throwing pennies into the Grand Canyon makes it a prairie. Especially Rachel. The abyss is too deep, and too vast, and praise from a posture of submission is so tiny that all it really does is make her see how impossibly insufficient you are."

"I don't know," I contend. "I guess it seems more like one of those things where you just hug the kid until the kid quits kicking and screaming and calms down. I see Rachel more like that — desperate for affirmation from a man who isn't just trying to get into her pants, who is strong enough to do better by her."

"Is that what you did with Betsy?" he asks.

"Yeah, pretty much. Except that a certain access to her pants was part of the deal."

"But in the end you weren't enough."

"I don't know if that's what the problem was."

"Okay." And he casually slackens his posture to show me that he's not going to push it further.

Betsy drove down from Chicago and spent last night with me at my parents' house. It had been a long time — and things have changed. I don't think we'll ever see each other again. We went to dinner and watched a movie together, but there was nothing for us to talk about. She didn't want to talk about our past or what happened, or about the other guy and how things were going with him, or about my world in Denver. She just wanted to be with me and hide in my kind words. I was the idol she pulled from her pocket for some cheap praise on her terms. And I did the same with her. It was hollow. Consumptive. Embarrassing. We were a match made in hell from the very beginning.

Finally, after a year of tortured conversations with Betsy, and neither of us being quite able to explain why we were still talking, but neither being able to explain exactly why we shouldn't, I know it's finished. Whatever we had before is gone, and frankly it's only sad the way never getting to play high school football again is sad. It's just over, a remnant from another time, and it didn't carry forward. The rules have changed. She's not the same person anymore, and neither am I. The people we both were before are gone, dead like anyone else in history. I knew it, and she seemed to know it to an extent, but it did still feel like we were getting something for free. It was affirmation and appreciation, but I felt like I was giving it from a place of honesty and abundance in myself — offering something real in exchange for something false. And worse than that, Betsy was offering something real of herself at the feet of a false projection of me. We didn't see each other at all. Had we ever? Had I ever seen anyone? Had I ever been seen?

"So what am I supposed to be, if not nice?" I ask Jon.

"You know, the opposite of nice is not mean. Nice is all about appearances and saying the right words — it's about offering yourself up for evaluation and critique and rejection from the other person.

Especially the way you describe it. The opposite of being nice is being authentic and openhanded with the power you wield over the other person. That's what you should be. That's what can fill a woman because it gives her something to hold onto, something to choose instead of what she would otherwise manipulate from you. If you are authentically yourself, even if you're a mess, it's a ton stronger than being the puppy dog with the soft coat and gentle words. You know why you haven't already had sex with Rachel and been passed along for the next *homme du jour*, as you call it?"

"No, Doctor. Why?" I've never thought about her flirtation actually involving sex with the guys who seemed to follow her everywhere. Am I being that guy — the guy who doesn't see what everyone else sees about the cute girl who's nice to him? Is that why David leaves the door open? Was I the last one to see it with Betsy? Oh, man.

"Because you haven't tried. You share the same personality deficit. You both want other people to make the first move to validate you, and neither of you really cares enough about offering something to the other person to risk making the move yourself. She'd say yes to you — it's part of the trade she offers guys. From what you've said, it's the same trade you make when you sit there being all nice until a woman makes the first move. She strikes her pose and asks, like all women seem to, 'Am I pretty?' and you strike your pose, on your knees begging, and ask with your nice guy voice, 'Am I nice? Am I insightful? Am I trustworthy and loyal and unthreatening enough that you're willing to use me for a cheap moment of escape? If *I'm* the one who tells you you're pretty, will you see me as man enough to believe it? Could I be your god?' And you sound just like every guy trained in the talk show generation."

I feel a bauble wiggle loose on my shell. A big one. I feel exposed. I feel a threat to my sense of value. I feel a threat to my lovability. It's a sick sensation. After maybe a minute I say, "Yeah."

"Hey, sorry I pushed. Sometimes I work too hard to make a point that doesn't really need to be made." And I can tell he really feels torn up about my response.

"No big deal. Good thoughts," I respond, though I have absolutely no idea what to think about Rachel, four car lengths in front of us and totally unaware of what's just been said about her. "How about another Mountain Dew?"

CHAPTER 19

As Honest As the Moment Is

For all of my concerns about the culture of Christian heroism, I still very much want to be a holy man. I want to do it for real, not for the stage. So I'm doing what it seems like a holy man would do. I pray and I study and I go to church, and I've taken a job as the pastor's assistant at Five Points Christian Church, which is in the downtown Denver neighborhood w here I used to go in hopes of getting shot. I'm the only white guy for a couple of blocks, and when I get off the light rail I pass crack dealers and prostitutes and homeless people — some of whom I've gotten to know by name. I've been learning a lot about racial reconciliation and about how it takes black women longer to dry their hair and how urban people really don't want to be white suburbanites. In Indianapolis I always pictured the inner city as a sort of fenced-in, free-for-all zone like I'd seen in movies about life after nuclear war, or after the robots took over. I assumed there was nothing I could do to make a difference downtown, and for the most part that was fine with me because I also believed that poor people were poor because they lacked the character to pull themselves up by their bootstraps, whatever those are, and it seemed like they'd stay poor only until they decided being poor sucked enough to stop being poor. I knew Zionsville was insulated and anomalous, but I didn't realize how far from the real world it is. Zionsville, and really the bulk of the khaki-and-denim-shirt white world, is in touch with reality the way any other fanatic with an idea, an ideal, and an idol is in touch with reality.

I have a guide through all of this, for whom I am grateful. His name is Ellison, and we met at seminary. His mother is white and his father is black, which is true of Ellison's wife as well. Ellison is a year older than I am and is the associate pastor for a white church in Boulder. He also does a fair amount of preaching in black churches around town, and it's happened more than once that I've attended those services and been asked, as a visitor, to stand up and introduce myself so the congregation can welcome me. I always say, "I go wherever I can still hear Ellison preach for free," and everyone laughs and he looks good. Ellison is also paid to spend a portion of his time at Five Points Christian, and we do quite a bit together.

The church building was built by a German congregation in 1892, and its steeple is visible for blocks. Only about twenty people attend services on Sunday, but maybe 150 come for a hot meal every Saturday afternoon, and about the same come to the food bank on Wednesdays. The house behind the church has been turned into a community center, where people come for bus passes or clothing for job interviews, or for help with things like a temporary mailing address, or to connect with other ministry assistance elsewhere. Pastor Arrington is the man over all of it, and I ask Ellison a lot of questions about the way he works. The Five Points Christian complex is all donated, and most of the donations are drawn out in this strange dance of white guilt and a laughing, shuffling performance from

Arrington. Oh, that laugh, though. It starts with a dry rasp, and then bounces its way louder with these coarse hooting sounds that lift his shoulders up to his ears as though the joy he's sharing with his companion is far more precious than the work that surrounds them. He creates something like a foxhole humor with it, where joy will not be scared off by the taxation of struggle and toil and despair at hand. And I suppose that is the truth of it; there really is good news to talk about even in the broken lives that pass through the church all the time. Pastor Arrington laughs easily like that with anyone, but there is something different about the way he does it with a white person dropping off a box of food or clothes or whatever. I can't tell if it's a remnant from a time where submission was expected, or if there's something else behind it.

"Is he putting on an act to keep the donations coming?" I ask Ellison over an out-of-season plastic cup of donated eggnog in the dining hall. "Is he that savvy and that willing to do what it takes to bring the best results for the people he serves?"

"What if he is?"

"That would suck. He's either not being respectful of himself, or he's being horribly disdainful of the donors. And it would mean that he's perpetuating several kinds of horrible stereotypes and roles."

"Whose fault is it if that works?"

"I think blaming white people for being clumsy in their efforts to help and making fools of them by playing a false role makes the gap between black and white that much greater, don't you?"

Ellison is staring absently at the eggnog carton. "What is 'nog,' anyway?"

"It's eggs, and cream, and sugar — "

"But what's 'nog'?"

I decide to play back. "You really don't know?"

"No."

"Well, I guess that's because you didn't grow up near farms. Eggnog is a German drink they serve around Christmas because that's when they also make sausage."

"Huh?"

"You know that sausage wrappers are really cleaned out intestines that are stuffed with meat, right?"

"Yeah."

"Nog is the yellow mucus lining they roll out of the intestines when they prepare them for stuffing." I show him the rolling action with my hands.

He squints at me, his lips coming apart slightly and curling down at the corners.

"Ellison, I don't know what the heck nog is," I say, laughing. "Tell me about the thing with Arrington and lying to white people."

"I wouldn't say he's lying."

"He's not being honest."

"He's being as honest as the moment is."

"What's dishonest about wanting to help people?"

"Nothing, if that's what it really is."

"Oh, geez," I say, feigning exhaustion. "Is this another complaint about the handout not being warm enough?"

"Beggars can't be choosers, right?" He tips his plastic cup at me, nodding a salute.

"When it comes down it to, that's exactly right," I respond, Republican sensibilities shining through. I can back this up scripturally too.

"And that's the gap in the moment. That's the piece that Arrington is being courteous about. He's interacting with people in a way that matches their side of the deal."

"What's the 'gap in the moment'? What's he being courteous about?" I pivot my thumbs up like I don't get what makes him think he just scored a point.

"When someone comes here to give to someone they call 'brother' because they're both Christians, the claim is that something better than throwing scraps to beggars is being done. Arrington is not a beggar; he's being called 'brother.' And the people Arrington helps are called brother, too, even if Arrington is the proxy for that brotherhood. The gap comes because stereotypical white people don't know the difference between helping a brother and helping a beggar — all need is weakness, and stereotypical white Christians get real uncomfortable around weakness. Arrington's willing to work with that discomfort. He thanks people in a way that makes them feel like they contributed something important, and he invites them back. It's the opposite of complaining that the handout isn't warm enough. It's recognizing that some people need the comfort of making sure the handout is cold to maintain a sense of distance from the weakness they perceive. He's not trying to change the attitudes of the people who donate; he's meeting them where they're at."

"But doesn't he have some obligation to do just that — to change the way donors see what they're doing?" I take a sip of eggnog, "If what they're doing is really wrong, that is."

Ellison knows this ground better than I do. "No. He has an obligation to make a choice about how he'll respond to being put in the role of beggar. Will he take what's being offered or not? That's the way beggars are choosers. The person doing their drive-by good deed isn't asking what he needs; they're saying, 'Here, take this.'"

This is frustrating for me. "Aren't the people who help just doing what they've been asked to do? It's not like they just spontaneously decided to bring groceries to some church downtown without knowing about the church and the programs here."

"Actually, sometimes that's exactly what happens. But you're right; most of the time people come because that's what their church has told them about the needs here. With some churches, that's all

Arrington tells them about. But you've been here a few weeks now; do you think more than food bank donations are needed?"

"Sure. Though I don't think there's enough of a structure to make good use of volunteers for much else."

Ellison points at me with a quick gun gesture. "Exactly. How do you communicate real needs through impersonal structures? It's hard to tell a suburban church, 'We need you to come down and meet some people and see what stirs in your heart. It will likely end up taking more time from your schedule than you were planning, and it may even be enough to upset large portions of your world. And while we can provide the introductions and give you some guidance as you go, we're not set up for you to just come in and volunteer for a couple of hours and then head back to suburbia.' That's too brother, not enough beggar. Beggars say, 'I need a dime.' They offer a binary yes or no opportunity to help. A brother says, 'I feel something's not right in my world.' It's messier, and many times there are no answers, and what matters is who's willing to spend his time sitting beside that brother. If someone who would be a healthy influence doesn't spend the time, there are always unhealthy people willing to hang out. The people who do their drive-by Christian duty are looking to do a good deed, to do something that absolves them of a sense of obligation, and Arrington is willing to be friendly and say, 'Thank you for the food. Please come back.'"

"They're just building goodwill for their personal brand."

"Uh, maybe. If you mean they're mostly motivated by making themselves feel good, then yes, though of course they also think they're doing more."

"Yeah, okay." I take a second, wanting to hold the floor, but not sure quite what I'm feeling. I go with a question I've had a long time. "You say that a lot of the time there aren't answers, but isn't that mostly a cop out for people who don't want to take the common sense steps they need to take to improve their lives? I mean, I see new coats on kids in the projects, or big TVs with cable there. Or the young single mothers who leave their kids at home while they go out partying and end up with more kids. Those are common sense things — obvious answers. It's not like poverty is some mystery."

Ellison stares at me for a moment. I can tell he's doing work walking me through all of this, and it's humbling. He finds a way to explain it. "There's a story where Jesus is near Jericho and a blind beggar hears it's Jesus passing by. He yells out, 'Son of David, have mercy on me!' So Jesus has the man brought to him in the crowd, and what do you think he does with the blind beggar next?"

I nod for him to get on with the story and say, "He restores the man's sight, of course."

"No. He asks, 'What do you want me to do for you?'"

"Yeah, and then he heals the guy."

"The beggar. He does heal him, but first he asks. It's entirely possible that the beggar could have said, 'I've been blind my whole life, and I get around fine. What I'm worried about is my bad leg, my sick wife, and my son who's been taken into slavery. Can you help with those things?' You're right that there are some simple changes people can make to change a great deal about their lives, but there is a critical difference between the way we treat beggars and the way we treat brothers. The difference between beggar and brother is asking the question."

"But you just said that all Arrington tells some churches about is the food bank type stuff. When someone asks what he needs, isn't that like what Jesus asked? When a suburban church asks what they can do to help, aren't they doing the same thing? Isn't that the moment when they prove that they want Arrington to be brother instead of beggar? Isn't it up to Arrington to give the real answer then?"

"Here's where things get complicated. For some churches, he does tell them about what he'd really like to see. He'll tell them about more long-term relationship stuff. And most of the time the pastor who's asking the question will say that's more than his congregation is likely to be willing to jump into, so they're left with the lowest common denominator stuff like serving food at the community meal or dropping off donations. Other pastors ask the question, but aren't really asking the question. They're mostly interested in adding to the list of good deed things and good idea partners their church has, and they're looking for a binary sort of help to toss Arrington's way, and they don't see much value in the relationship beyond what they can bring downtown. It's a hard thing to know which pastor is which, and it's a rare thing to have someone be willing to come down here and sit and learn. I'm sure there are times when Arrington doesn't give the real answer because he doesn't feel optimistic about the response that will come."

"So he goes with what people assume he'll need because that's the way donors are used to helping."

"Yeah. And he needs food for the food bank."

CHAPTER 20

A COLLECTION OF ONE

"You have such beautiful hair. Don't you think his hair is beautiful, Sister Hazel?" I'm at the community center behind Five Points Christian Church, and the center's director, a middle-aged black woman with long fingernails and cigarette breath, has her hands, both hands, in my hair. "It's so soft and so fine."

Sister Hazel responds, "It sure is, Miss Gladys."

"I wish my hair was like this," Miss Gladys gushes.

I finish making photocopies and head back over to the church office. I feel odd. I don't want to stand out. I don't want to have one more thing that a black person does not. I look around at the world down here, and I see so much that makes me ashamed of the world I'm from. I see people enduring each other's pain, finding room enough for it to be matter-of-fact, as pain and failure truly are. I see genuine warmth and honest sacrifice. I see older women taking in foster children and carefully parenting them. I see grown women call each other "Sister" and "Miss," and I feel the respect that comes with those words. I watch the way people who come to the hot meals or to the food bank or to the community center are legitimately grateful for the service they receive. There's a ministry down the street where a man — a white guy with a long beard that inspired me to grow the one that has bushed out red and curly — opens a storefront coffeehouse at five in the morning because the liquor stores open at six and he wants to give the homeless alcoholics a place to choose mercy on whichever morning the desire for sobriety finally grabs them. That man keeps the alley behind his storefront swept and clean because he knows the men he serves sleep there. A couple of nights ago one uninitiated homeless man shattered a bottle against the wall, and the other homeless men beat him up for it, then made him clean up the space to show a little respect. I've been at lunch down the street and seen Crips, gang members in their blue kerchiefs, take the kerchiefs off of their heads to pray before they eat. There is something about the pain and the hardship in the world down here that makes ordinary life so sweet, so rich, and I don't want to have anything to do with holding up Zionsville or soft blond hair as something to be envied. I don't like that I represent a false idol about life just for the way I look. I know it's an overstatement to say that something, anything, about the way I'm living, earning less than my rent and eating from the food bank, sells suburbia or will make people down here feel badly about their lot, but there is something in me that wants to be rid of my own connections to my escape route, to the duality I feel.

A couple of hours later there's a knock on the front door of the church, which remains closed and locked when there are not services going on. Pastor Arrington looks up from his papers and I answer the door. There is a filthy white guy in his forties standing there.

"How you doing?" I ask him.

"Not so good, not so good. It's supposed to snow tonight, and I'm trying to scrape together some cash to get indoors. Can you help me out?"

He's lying.

"Sorry," I say, "but we don't give cash. I can make sure there's room for you at the shelter if you want, and I can hook you up with a bus pass."

"No, that's okay. But hey, can I get a couple of bucks from you to buy some food?"

He's still lying. He wants the cash so he can buy something to get high.

"I have a pass to get me home," I tell him, "and that's all I've got on me. But we do have some food in the pantry, and I'd be happy to grab some for you."

"No, thanks." He's ready to walk away.

"Tell you what I will do, though," I say. "I'll make you a trade."

"For what?"

"All you've got are those beat-up sneakers?"

"Yeah."

"Those holes are going to suck when it snows."

"Yeah."

"I'll trade you these new boots for your shoes. My mom just bought them for me about a month ago."

"Yeah, okay. Sure." And he starts slipping them off. He knows not to ask if there's a catch. Maybe he doesn't care. Maybe he knows there isn't one. I untie my boots and we hand each other our footwear.

"Hey, these are nice," he says.

"Good. And they'll be warm. Sorry I couldn't help with the money, but I hope you'll come back if there's anything else you need. You know about the meal on Saturday, right?"

"Yeah. Hey, man, thanks." He offers his hand and we shake hands, white style. I close the door and return to the office, dropping his shoes in the trash.

"What was that?" Pastor Arrington asks.

"Just helping a brother out," I reply.

"With your shoes?" he asks.

"It's what he needed," I respond. Pastor Arrington grunts a little and returns to his work. So do I, and nothing more is said.

The workday ends in the late afternoon and I lock the door as I leave, shoeless, coat collar up to my ears. I walk the three blocks to the light rail, watching the ground for glass or needles, but I don't encounter any to avoid. People at the rail stop look at me curiously, noticing my socks. The light rail takes me to the transfer station near the college where I catch my bus. People notice again. And I start thinking again about the collector crab, about how we go through our lives with a certain list of traits or comebacks or whatever that we rely upon to tell us, or others if need be, why we're good enough to be in a certain situation. The collection is our idol, and it's everything to us. I usually notice the dynamic when I walk into a physician's waiting room, where other people are already waiting, and it seems obvious that the first thing people try to figure out is what each other's illnesses are. When I walk into those sorts of situations I find myself reviewing a list of things like, "I'm smart. I'm educated. I have some money. I'm kind. I know some martial arts in case I have to fight." Sitting on the bus it occurs to me that all of that is wiped away in strangers' eyes by the fact that I don't have any shoes on. For the first time I see how truly silly every item on my list of qualifications is, how easily the shell can be scraped bare.

We get to my stop, and people watch me as I disembark. There is glass on the sidewalk in front of the lots next door to the condo I've rented with Jon, and I tread carefully. And then I stop. The mountains are already white with the snow that's coming, but there is a break in the clouds and the sky is a beautiful red and yellow and purple smear. I have only one qualification, and it's the one I forget about almost as soon as I remember it, when I do remember it. I have no claim to worthiness, on a bus or at a community center or anyplace else, but instead of the bottomless well of my sin, I have the love of Jesus who says I'm okay, and that makes me okay. I have only Jesus to excuse me or to make me worth knowing. Everything else is just silliness. I stand and sing quietly to the sunset:

"Praise God from whom all blessings flow.

Praise him all creatures here below.

Praise him above ye Heavenly host.

Praise Father, Son, and Holy Ghost."

Jesus is my only protection, my only source of self. I head inside and shave my head, leaving my bushy red beard untouched, to remind me of the beauty and necessity of a shell only covered by my Lord.

CHAPTER 21

Chocolate and Bible Study

Jon and I have been going to a cool downtown church called Church in the City — a place I attended while I was in school because the last thing I needed on Sunday was another lecture. Pastor Arrington has no problem with my attending other churches on Sundays, so long as I'm on time at Five Points the rest of the week. It turns out a large group of people from Church in the City, maybe forty or fifty who are about our age and place in life, meet in what's called the "college and career" class. It's a lame name, but several of the girls are very good-looking, so when we're invited to attend a home Bible study, Jon accepts for us.

The group meets in the upstairs apartment of an old house in a rough part of town. Our first visit starts off about the way such events always go: cookies and chips in bags, ice from the store, two-liter bottles of soda to be poured into plastic cups and carried into the mismatched living room of futons, poster art, a television on a crate, and the obligatory single plant fighting for survival in the corner near the drafty window. Jon gets a seat on a futon, and I end up on the floor, shifting my weight as my butt and legs fall asleep.

The people are friendly. The church is big on growth and inviting new people, and Jon's good looks and interesting way of talking bring him attention. I get the double effort: the normal one that strangers extend unattractive strangers, plus the added quick-nodding cheerleader-like enthusiasm that nice people offer someone whose harder-to-categorize bald head and beard make him look like the photo negative of Gordon from *Sesame Street*.

After some mingling, the host, Twan, a guitar-playing struggling actor a few years older than everyone else, prays to officially open the evening. Then he throws out the icebreaker topic. "Tonight we're going to talk about temptation. The Bible says that Jesus was faced with all of the temptations we know, and because he experienced them, he is able to be a better, more understanding judge of what our lives are like. I thought maybe we could go around the room and each share what our own biggest temptations are, and then move into the study."

If I've ever experienced a perfect example of the absolute loss of contact with the real world that exists in much of the Church today, it's in Twan's question. Our biggest temptations? As an icebreaker? In a quick trip around a circle on futons over Safeway grape soda and Chips Ahoy? I sigh. I know how this is going to go.

Joanie is first, because Twan gestures for her to start.

"I guess it's probably procrastinating."

"Oooh. Good one," Becky says.

"That was mine," Kathy echoes. "I'm so bad about that."

"What about you, Kirk?" Twan continues.

"I think TV takes a lot of my life," he replies. There are nods.

Crissy, the bubbly, granola, Meg Ryan-esque nurse who wears her blue hospital scrubs at all times, is next. "Chocolate. Absolutely chocolate."

That is Holly's, too, though she doesn't say so to the group. She turns to Joanie the Procrastinator and their body language makes clear the jealousy and bitterness the two heavier girls have toward Crissy and the attention she gets from the men in the group. The men, to Holly's point, respond to Crissy with things like:

[Antonio] "If that's your sin, it sure doesn't show."

[Twan] "Better be careful — someone could use that against you." Wink.

[Robert] "You know, chocolate's an aphrodisiac."

And as soon as he says it, Robert, who looks like Niles from the show *Frasier*, skinny with thinning blond hair and the careful walk of a clarinet player in a marching band, shrinks back a little. He's obviously not the sort to say such things. Jon and I may are the only people in the room to catch what he said. We looked at each other and smiled. A new friendship is born.

The next person in the circle is Pamela, a dark-haired Swiss woman who looks and dresses like a slender single mother in love with a rock star. In fact, she is a single mother, to a three-year-old, and her ex-husband is in jail for something to do with cocaine. Twan scrapes his eyes off Crissy to turn the question about temptation to Pamela.

"What about you?" he asks.

"I think you're all full of it," she says. "I like chocolate, and I would watch too much television if I could, but the truth is that what we really want is to be having sex."

There are guffaws and squeals and gasps and furrowed brows everywhere. But she continues.

"I want chocolate, but I want it melted and licked off me. Several times. And so do all of you. Maybe in front of the television. And Joanie, even you wouldn't put that off until tomorrow."

Twan is desperate to regain control of the moment. "Well, I'd say the ice is sufficiently broken!" And he steers the discussion to the notes he's printed out. As we file out at the end of the evening, he pulls Pamela aside and tells her that he understands it was her first time to the study, but that her answer had been inappropriate, especially in mixed company.

That's Christian culture in a nutshell. We have this Bible that tells horrible stories about sin and depravity and temptation and addictions that overwhelm people, even to death. And we pray to this God who loves us and mourns for our suffering and yearns to clean us up, set us free, and draw us to him — and not necessarily in that order. And we have Jesus who sought out and spent his time hanging with people who laughed too loudly, who were surely not tea party material, and who were very often absolutely buried in inappropriate behaviors and lifestyles. Jesus preferred them because they were not the religious "whitewashed tombs," painted and clean on the outside, but dead and reeking on the inside.

Christianity has this entire worldview that treats the filth of life as impermanent, redeemable, escapable, and unable to make the bride too filthy to be loved. But we have this thing in our culture where we don't believe a bit of it. We work so overly hard to make God look good that what we say has no credibility at all; we lie about him all the time. We're such cow-brained dullards. In our insecurities and arrogance, and our lack of honesty, we demand to see God turn lives around, to do something cool for us. To be our dancing poodle. We want to be able to tell a great story about how well our lives have been transformed by this God who, to our exquisite torture, simply does not do enough flashy stuff for us to feel comfortable letting his work stand on its own. We are so desperate to share the good news that we almost always fake it. We forge the miraculous and we promise more than we really experience ourselves. And we are so conflicted about how to be "good Christians" — people whose lives have been turned around and made squeaky clean — even though that's not what we experience exactly, that we have developed a twisted, hand-wringing culture where we are far less matter-of-fact about sin and temptation and doubt and the profane than are our Scriptures, our God, or even the rest of the world around us where there is no promise of rescue or redemption. We're obnoxious fools, and our dishonesty makes us incredibly vulnerable and weak — and far from trustworthy to people who could actually benefit from knowing the truth according to God.

It's frustrating that there's no way I'd be able to tell "good Christians" about my life in any sort of real terms, and mine has been exceedingly tame and safe. I can only imagine how people with darker closets must feel. If I wanted to talk about my life, I'd have to make veiled references, using terms that demonstrated that my sins had passed through the evangelical autoclave and been sterilized. It would be important that I didn't use any of the naughty words, and that every evidence of past evil wore a nice pink bow of present righteousness. I'd hear about the passage in James that talks about coarse talk and how fresh water and salt water cannot flow in the same stream, or about Ephesians where Paul writes that it's shame to even speak of the sins people do in darkness.

I'm not interested in being slave to or defined by my sins. I'm not looking to be a hero for them. I don't even want to hold onto them. But certainly there must be some way for me to make sense of my sins, to learn what is true in the face of the pain and confusion and lack of control I've known. Isn't there? And I can think of dozens of really nasty stories in the Bible, about a woman driving a tent spike through a man's head into the ground, or about a king — a man "after God's own heart," no less — who sees a woman bathing and later sends her husband to certain death so the king can cover up the fact that he's already knocked her up, or about Jesus taking and eating wheat from another man's field on the Sabbath when all of the good religious people were scandalized by such forbidden behavior. Beyond those are a whole assortment of stories about rape, incest, adultery, idolatry, murder — everything. If there is a point to the experiences in the Bible, if those stories mean something when held up to the light of God, why wouldn't it make sense for me, or anyone else, to do the same?

I think Pamela's comment during the Bible study was perfect. In fact, if there was a problem, it was treading so naively on ground made sacred by the battle between good and evil for the prize of our souls and sanctification. My battles and my temptations are hard places, bloody and filthy places, sacred places, where the image of God I bear is under significant attack. It is a holy place, and it is not a trivial pursuit. If you're going to wander where the cows graze, you'd better be ready to get your shoes dirty.

CHAPTER 22

Don't Know What to Say About Poverty

This morning I woke up five days away from my next paycheck. In the meantime, I have one cup of uncooked beans, one cup of uncooked rice, and just over four dollars to my name. I am officially a "poor person," and I don't like it and I don't like how it disorients me.

Here's what I've always thought: Poor people are poor because they make poor choices, meaning either bad choices or the immediate gratification choices commonly associated with the poor. The family may be in jeopardy of having the electricity turned off, but there is a nice TV in the family room and at least one of the kids is wearing some name-brand coat or shoes with Michael Jordan on them. The hand that's trading food stamps for groceries seems to forever have a fancy manicure. Jobs are scarce, but there's always cash for cigarettes and alcohol. Birth control is somehow perceived by a single mother as more expensive than another baby. Being a deadbeat dad sleeping on the couch at a friend's house is no big deal so long as the pager stays on and a man can still get some action at the club. I've always thought poverty comes down to weak, selfish, short-term choices made in the face of wiser options.

But today I'm questioning if it's really true that poor choices are the same thing as weak choices. Could it be that sometimes they're self-affirming choices, albeit stolen and taxed heavily by consequence, but noble in their own way? Are there times when even people who are being wise about their poverty reach the end of the patience and humility it takes to manage their suffering?

And it is suffering. In a world where having things and being able to do things is presented as the norm, and where so many people nearby have so many more resources, poverty in America comes with a very distinct and oppressive feeling of being a second-class citizen. And actually, poverty is pretty much how we distinguish between first- and second-class citizenship. We're not so concerned with worth, inherent though our Constitution may proclaim it; we measure people by economic utility. If your net worth isn't worth much, neither are you. Certainly there are places in the world, pretty much everyplace else, actually, where poverty is far worse. But there are few places where the distinction in lifestyle between people with means and people without is as crisp and tightly spaced as it is here, and where the poor are shown so clearly what they don't have. The feeling of self-denial that comes with being a good steward of poverty's wages is a huge, numbing weight that is very definitely a sort of suffering.

I've been good about it for the roughly one hundred twenty days I've been working at Five Points Christian — living on few dollars and food bank food. Granted, my type of poverty is chosen, and I can push the "No Thanks" button anytime I want and return to the life from which I've come. I can go get the job, buy the house and car, and walk away. I've probably felt the suffering in a more sudden and acute way than people who grow up with it, but I've also felt it in a far more superficial and temporary way, and have certainly not experienced the soul-warping (or refining, depending who you ask) weight of chronic poverty.

I've eaten the beans, rice, and other donated food I've carried home from work, and felt guilty eating it because I know the donors didn't have people like me in mind when they gave. I've even spent the couple of dollars it costs me to take the bus and train back to Five Points Christian to get a hot Saturday lunch at the soup kitchen. When I gave away my boots, David and Danielle bought me new ones from their modest budget, and I felt selfish and silly for playing this poverty game and taking from them. I've felt the desire to be able to buy my own things, or to eat what I want. I've missed Chicago, where I could get a free meal just for working late, or where on more than one occasion I bought new clothes so I wouldn't have to do laundry.

But there's a piece of me, a piece that has always allowed me an arm's length buffer zone of arrogant distance between myself and poor people and their poor choices, that I can feel crumbling. And frankly, it's terrifying; I don't want to be like ... them.

I have no room on my credit cards, and once that bit of food and cash runs out, I'll either have to wait or beg for more. It was the first thing I thought of when I woke up, as I would assume it is often the first thing people with very little wake up considering. And I felt it more than I thought it. I felt like I was at the end of my options. I felt weak. I felt as though I had been foolish. I felt as though I deserved to be in crisis, because that is what I've always thought of people who were not heavily entrenched in Crown Ministries or some other stewardship system. Fortunately, I'd already purchased my bus pass for the week, so I will get to work with no hit to my pocketbook.

I'm standing in the aisle because there are no seats on the bus, and I think about my bald head under the mud cloth kufi I've started wearing. I consider my identity in Christ, and I remember that he is my provider, and I cannot forget how much worse things must be for people in real poverty. I pray for them, and I pray about my own stuff, both financially and emotionally. I thank God that he is pulling me through a challenging time and that I am learning something from the discomfort. We pass a billboard for Egg McMuffins, and I nearly tear up.

Money, food, success, impact, opinions of family or friends — all idols, forever cycling through my attention, forever with short-lived protection, and forever with eventual disappointment. There must be something better than being a collector crab. Something better than hiding behind this mix of qualifications. It's Jesus, right? My one thing? I've been bought at a price. I've been claimed. I belong to him and he ascribes my identity to me. He is the way, the truth, and the life. Not a way, a truth, or a life, but *the* way, *the* truth, and *the* life. No one comes to the Father but through the Son. It must be that Jesus is my one thing, my single protection, my strong tower, my hiding place. My collection is a collection of trash. My collector crab is dead.

I'm the only one on the bus thinking this stuff.

There's another kind of crab in the *schizophroida* genus. It's called the sponge crab. Where the collector crab attaches a variety of things to its shell, the sponge crab uses its pincer claws to trim off a piece of living sponge exactly the size of its shell. Sort of an all-your-eggs-in-one-basket strategy. The sponge crab uses two specially formed hind legs to hold the sponge in place, like a hat in the wind. If you put a sponge crab with its sponge hat in a tank with a squid, the squid will stay away because the sponge is toxic to it. The crab doesn't have to hide. It does not have to blend into its surroundings for safety. It can stand out; it can be a stranger in a strange land. It can move boldly, immune to the attacks of the squid. It can be Batman with his cape, Wonder Woman with her bracelets, me with my piece of living Jesus bouncing along on my back. I can't even begin to picture what it would be like to live without fear — to know that Jesus will protect me if I let him. Incredible.

Could it be as easy for me to hold Jesus as it is for a crab to hold a sponge? Would sin want to stay away from righteousness as much as a squid would want to stay away from the toxin? Am I as naturally inclined to grasp my Savior as the crab is inclined to cling to its savior? Yes! I hold Jesus to me like a hat in the wind, and I press on. There is but one name under heaven to whom all will bow — and I don't have to pronounce it correctly or with a seminarian's doctrinal precision for the name to offer its protection.

Of course, if you take the sponge away, the crab is dead meat.

If I lose Jesus, I'm hosed.

Plus: If you offer the crab something other than sponge, like a rubber sandal or a piece of paper, it will trim the sandal or the paper exactly to the size of its shell and hold it in place like a hat in the wind. A misled sponge crab will eagerly put all of its hope in the wrong defense. It's naturally inclined to find, trim, grasp, and confidently move beneath the protection of the sponge — its idol, its god; but it doesn't have the capacity to recognize true safety from false.

Some days all I see are squids, and I find myself hoping that I'm really clinging to the right thing. After all, once the sponge is on your shell you can't see it anymore. But I tell myself it'd be foolish to risk double-checking what I've put on my shell. I'd be exposed. Besides, if I couldn't pick out the right protection the first time, why would I expect to get it right this time? No, I can't admit there's a chance I've put a false sponge on my shell or I'll never trust my protection again. Better to keep going and not talk or think about it.

And then I remember that a sponge crab holding a sandal or a paper hat on its shell is just as tasty to a squid as a sponge crab with no defense of any kind.

How do I know if what I've understood, trimmed, and donned is the man and not just a symbol of Jesus? What if I'm holding onto only the stuff I want about him, and not taking him also as my master and God or whatever else I don't want about him?

A couple of things give me pause about the sponge crab. First, the sponge remains alive and growing, but it doesn't grow as quickly as the crab; so a time comes when the crab has to replace its sponge, and during that period the crab is quite vulnerable. How do you know when you've outgrown your sponge? I know more of Jesus now than I did when I first arrived in Denver, but I'm still not good at letting him be him — it's too much for me. I still find myself trimming off the portions of him that I can understand, grasp, and control. How do you know when the portion of Jesus you've trimmed and clasped to your head has become too small for your growing self? How do you know when the Jesus you thought you saw as you cut him loose from the impossibly large mass of God has become inadequate — not defense or even placebo, but mere superstition? How do you know when you've outgrown the Jesus you were facing when you first offered yourself to him? The smallest prison in the world is a faith that doesn't let Jesus grow.

The second thing about the sponge crab is that it is only as safe as its grip on the sponge — and the more it outgrows the sponge, the more it'll have to stretch to reach across its shell with its special legs. I know that I'm growing, and growth causes confusion about answers I used to feel so confident hiding beneath. And the smaller my image of Jesus gets in relation to my life's experiences, the harder it is for me to maintain my grip on him. If my life grows in ways that my faith does not, then my grip will grow clumsier and less capable. There's something disquieting about my safety only being as dependable as my grip. I mean, how often does the crab see the squid coming, anyway? How does the crab know when to hold on tight?

One final freaky thing: the sponge has no particular concern for the crab. I know Jesus is very concerned with me, but what is he willing to let me experience when I mistake the protection of the portion of him I can control — the portion that I make into an idol — for the real thing? Many will come to him on that day and say, "Lord, Lord, did we not ..."

And he will say, "Depart from me — I never knew you."

The bus arrives at the light rail station, and the train takes me downtown, where I get off a couple of stops early. I feel like walking and being late to work. I pass and exchange greetings with a crack dealer named Eights who always wears football jerseys with the number eighty-eight on them. He sells the rocks for five and ten dollars, depending on what you're willing to do to earn the discount. When we first started talking, we threw jabs at each other for our lifestyle choices. Since then, we've gotten bored with that and have realized there's not much to say to one another, so we either nod at each other or trade "S'up?"s.

The crows on the wires near Five Points Christian call down at me as I make my way to the church. Today the battle feels real, and the taunting gives me deep chills.

All morning I watch the people come and go from the church. I watch the way Pastor Arrington has a special place of rank in the community. There's another pastor from elsewhere in the city who drives a bright green Rolls-Royce — for his people. When I first heard that last bit, I thought it was total garbage, but what I've come to understand is that in some cultures, unlike the suburban white culture I'm from, the community can feel a certain camaraderie with the person who reaches highest among them. In the case of the black pastor with the green Rolls-Royce, he represents the community's ability to drive the best, show up anywhere, and wield a certain voice and power that the people from within the community don't have on their own. In many ways he is their proxy, their emissary, their moderating priest in contact with the practical gods of power and privilege and progress. He is the Goliath in their army, the giant who can be sent out to fight to spare the lives of many others.

And even with communities or churches where there is no Goliath, as at Five Points Christian Church, there is a still a champion, a David, who is accorded a voice and a position of respect higher than that of the people. Champions are one of the few assets poor people have that white people like myself simply cannot see, and disenfranchised white people suffer for not having. The best we manage to create are heroes, and that's hardly the same thing. A hero is measured by how far above the people he rises. A champion is measured by how far the people lift him.

This morning I put my beans in water to soak before I left for work, and on the ride home I think about them. The skins will be floating on the top, as will some of the beans. I've always suspected floating beans are bad, but I've never known, so I've always just left them. The water will be cold, and the condo will be empty. Clean, but empty. Clean, and new, and white with vertical blinds and a gas fireplace on a light switch. Clean and convenient, with a 7-Eleven through the garage and across the alley, but empty. I'll be alone. I get to my stop and am halfway past the Burger King when the smell of the grill catches me. The light inside is yellow and warm. There are sliced, juicy tomatoes inside, on thick buns that soak up the burger grease. And mayonnaise and fries with ketchup. It's just a combo meal. Anyone can afford a combo meal. It's under four dollars. I can afford a combo meal. But if I buy one, I'll be left with nothing but my beans and rice for four-and-a-half days. The beans and rice won't get me through. I'll have to eat nothing for at least one full day. I guess that's no big deal; I've fasted as many as twenty-four days before. But I've never missed a meal I didn't want to miss. It would be a foolish choice to buy the burger. Better to make the beans and rice and use the four dollars on other cheap food. But anyone can afford a combo meal. I should be able to afford a combo meal. I'm sick of being at the end of my cash rope. Forget it. I'm going to buy the combo meal.

It is so nice and warm inside the restaurant, but I can't soak it up. I can't let myself enjoy this indulgence because I know it is foolish. It is a poor decision. I order the Whopper Combo meal with a regular Pepsi and its extra calories of sustenance, and I take a seat in the corner, not even removing my coat. I eat and feel like one of the people I see riding the bus for warmth. I hunch over my food, stealing my absurd measure of temporary validation. And the moment is over in an instant. I leave the tray on the trashcan and head back out into the cold to walk the rest of the way home with nothing but coins to my name.

In the Bible when people get really scared, they say they are "undone." I trudge from the Burger King feeling defeated, broken, confused. Undone. I don't know who I am. I don't know what to use as evidence of my identity. Of my worth. My weak crab legs lost their grip on the sponge at the first pressure of a combo meal, on the first day of using the metaphor.

My collection has failed me. My sponge has failed me.

Has Jesus? Have I failed myself? Is this just "one of those things" that happen because sin exists in the world? Is God that out of control? The hamburger sits heavy and greasy in my gut. I taste the onion on my breath. I want to cry. I feel spun and disoriented. I feel cracked and exposed. Weak. Worthless. Betrayed, but I don't want to think about that word because it makes me feel like I'm being ungrateful—like that's suddenly a trait I've never exhibited. If my family saw me they'd never want a piece of this adventure, of this "joy" that still exists beneath the mess. This is not their idea of a holy adventure worth abandoning everything to have. I don't know what happened. I don't know how to defend myself. I don't know where I could hide, or behind what. All I know is that the squid got me.

As I reach the front walk of my condo, a woman from seminary named Jenny, an acquaintance at best, is heading back to her car from my front door. She hurries back to the door to retrieve the envelope with which she greets me.

"Hi," she says. "My husband and I were praying about you last night, and we want you to have this. It's not much, but the Lord put you on our hearts and we felt like we were supposed to tell you to hang in there. It's fifty dollars." She gives me a quick hug.

I'm stunned. "Would you like to come in?"

"No, I can't. I'm late for class already. Maybe we can have you over for dinner sometime soon, though?"

"Yeah," I say, totally disoriented. "Thank you. And thank you for the money too. It really means a lot to me."

I watch her drive away and then go inside.

CHAPTER 23

I'll Be Home for Christmas ... I Guess

Christmas. I'm in Zionsville. The descent into Indianapolis was turbulent, but I made the most of it by talking to the man in the seat next to me about wind shear and winter lightning to scare him. He'd been drinking too much and talking too much for most of the flight, and it was cheap revenge. I hate when people talk to me on flights, even more than I hate the stinky grape bubble gum I usually chew loudly and blow to annoy my neighbors enough so that they won't talk to me. It has to do with having strangers hear what I'm saying and murmuring things about how stupid or arrogant I am, same as I do when I listen to strangers talking. I forgot the gum this time, so I was left with only storytelling revenge.

That's pretty much the attitude I have about being home in general, and I don't like the person I'm being. There will be new sweaters and themed holiday jewelry on my brother and his fiancée. She'll end up in some silly turf squabble with my other brother's girlfriend, who is pretty much her exact opposite, except that they're both very competitive and want to be the favorite. For my part, I'll be Grandma's date whenever there is seating to figure out, and that will be the joke. That one stings, because I always thought I'd be married by now, and it's sure looking like I'll be third, if I end up married at all.

Mom will have made Norwegian potato tortillas called *lefsa*, representing her side of the family, and German fruit *kuchen* for my dad's. Both will be served with country sausage shipped frozen from the Red Owl in Wishek, North Dakota, where Dad spent his childhood. There will be consumption on top of consumption, and suburban genuflecting in front of the Christmas tree and again later at the midnight church service that will open with a hired orchestra and end with oil lamps and "Silent Night." Everyone will be dressed in their finest, and the holiday will strain hard to create moments of Wonderful Life. Hey, whatever keeps you from jumping off the bridge, George Bailey.

I'm being a jerk, I know. My parents throw up their hands and laugh when they see my shaved head and beard. They're very concerned about me, say I don't look well, ask if I've thought about taking multivitamins. My brothers joke about how I sold my computer and blew through my savings, joke about my being a Jesus freak.

I guess I am one, too. I am all about my one thing, my Jesus, my sponge, my single hope and single defense and only remaining answer, even if I have no idea what that answer really looks like. That makes me extremely weird. In Denver I've gotten rid of pretty much everything I own. I sleep on the floor on a sleeping bag. I gave away nearly all of my clothes, books, and music. I do my laundry in the bathtub, and recently I've been told I don't do it very well, which creates a keen paranoia in me about being the stinky fat guy. I pray and I read and I talk about God, and I am very aware of how Zionsville is not awake, how it's wallowing in its wealth and refuses to look at the world beyond it. I am exceedingly tiring to my parents in this regard, and so I tend to spend a lot of time quietly disgusted and fuming about the gluttony here, even as I keep finding myself taking a second helping of whatever's on the table or the television. Jesus freak, and a total jerk. I wish the two didn't come up as a pair so much of the time.

It's just that there is so much more. There are so many taboos here, questions that will upset the applecart and maybe bring some reassessment of life — and nobody cares. Just a bunch of frogs in a pot, the temperature on their souls rising, and the damage is already happening. It's so easy for me to slip right back into it, and that terrifies me. I thought I was fine when I was in Chicago, and before that too. I thought I knew how life was supposed to unfold and what it was about and what the right balances were between job and family and church and golf and vacations and retirement and, yes, maybe a mission trip or two and maybe a starving kid on the refrigerator. Leather seats feel good. New stereos sound good. Nice clothes, too, and nice cars. Cute candles and knickknacks and thoughtful gifts and comforting books. Coffee after an elegant dinner. A Scotch after a hard day at work. Burgers on the backyard grill. Bootstraps and tough love and trickle-down theories and all boats floating on a rising tide and loyalty to the contemporary interpretations of traditional values and the American Dream. I get it — I spent most of my life a spoiled recipient of the comforts of such a clichéd world. College didn't cost me a dime — other than what I earned during the summer to buy beer. It's a siren song, a world of lotus eaters. I want it, but it's all poison. And it makes unreal people out of all of us who consume it.

The world just isn't the way Zionsville wants it to be. And while I'd never advocate ruining what the wealthy have earned by taking it from them to give to the poor who have not earned it, there is a whole world full of volitional sacrifice and generosity that holds the promise of both sides sleeping well at night. And I don't think a soul in Zionsville gives two shakes about the fact that a sacrificial life, not just the portfolio, could be far better and far more satisfying than this life, parading indolently down wide streets of professionally serviced lawns in dark-windowed SUVs and minivans.

I'm a Jesus freak because I want something better. I want to recognize that how I live and what I consume does impact the people around me by modeling the wrong things on one hand or causing them to stumble in their envy on the other. I'm a Jesus freak because I'm willing to encourage people to take a sober look at their lives and ask if they're really happy. Really?

And that's the worst thing you can do in Zionsville.

CHAPTER 24

"I'd Like 'Things That Suck' for 500, Alex"

As much as anything, my frustration with Zionsville is fueled by how alone I feel in what I'm doing. How unsupported. I shouldn't be as unusual doing this sort of thing as I feel.

It's hard for me to live on dollars that show up miraculously to allow me to eat and do laundry. I'm ashamed of myself because I find that I can't do it without stealing hero points to keep me going. I'm angry because this is the right thing to be doing, and it requires more faith and more strength than I have.

I'm angry because I'm small, and because I'm a frightened crab.

Rachel called one night and said that she had come to understand that I couldn't give her what she wanted. I've been cool toward her for six months now, mostly focusing on not working for the nice guy compliments I get from her, and trying not to think about what happens with the other guys. She was frustrated and sad, and just about insane that her attempts to provoke me into professing my love for her didn't work. We still hang out pretty often, but we don't talk about deep personal things or about relationships. I have a huge crush on her, but I know we'd be a car wreck together. I've mostly become the guy she calls when she needs company to watch a movie or go to the bookstore. Hooray, me. Again.

Betsy called to tell me she'd gotten engaged. She called two days later to tell me she'd called it off and broken up. She wanted me to cheer her up. She was at her parents' house, and one of her brothers picked up the phone while we were talking. When she told him she was talking to me, he asked why she'd be talking to "that fat pig." I think maybe Betsy and I have been telling our stories differently.

My dad spent the rest of the time I was home making jabs about bleeding hearts, and I responded with comparisons to Rush Limbaugh. We laughed bitterly at each exchange. There was a lot of vinegar, very little honey, and no flies were caught by either side.

My brothers' significant others got into some dispute, and my brothers got sucked into it, too, so we didn't see each other the last few days I was around.

Lightning — in the last week of December — blew a hole in my condo wall several days before I returned to Denver from Indy. It didn't start a fire, but it did allow the room to get cold enough for some pipe to freeze and flood the place, which ruined the ceiling. That, and Jon turning the thermostat off instead of just down when we left Denver, gave us plenty to discuss with our landlord.

Before I left Zionsville, my mother asked me if I ever heard from Ivy, the woman who told me I should return to advertising in Chicago. I said I had not, and when I asked where the question was coming from, she said there was no reason.

So it was an odd coincidence that there was an envelope from Ivy waiting for me when I arrived at my soggy apartment, feeling like a champ. Inside the envelope was an article discussing a highly rated television show I'd never watched. The headline and theme were about the rise of family friendly programming and a resurgence in morality. I didn't read the article. I didn't really get past the note. It read simply, "God calls us to make a difference. When will you choose to do something worthwhile with your life?"

David's laughing at how things piled up. "Man, when it rains it pours with you, doesn't it?"

"Yeah, it's a riot," I say. We met for breakfast and have been in the vinyl booth long enough that we just ordered lunch. And something like an eighth refill on the Mountain Dews.

"Are you really thrown by the article?" he asks.

"Well, yeah. I mean, tell me you wouldn't be offended by something like that."

"Who cares what she thinks? She cares about media stuff, and she wants you to be a part of what she's doing. It's a compliment, if you think about it. At least she thinks you have something to offer."

"What I'm doing is not a waste of my life. It is making a difference. She doesn't see that. She has credibility with my parents, and I know that she must be talking to them."

"Ah, that."

"Yeah, that."

"Did I ever tell you the story about W.C. Fields and his love of the circus?"

"No."

"I'm not sure it's true, but it's a story my mentor told me a couple of years ago when I was feeling like I wasn't going to be able to provide for Danielle like her parents would hope."

"Okay."

"Well, as a kid W.C. loved the circus. He would watch the caravan roll in, spend days watching the elephants and the workers setting up the tent, would go to as many shows as he could, and would sneak into ones when he didn't have money, which was most of the time. He promised himself that if he ever he got rich, he'd make sure that any kid who wanted to go to the circus would be able to go."

"Nice guy," I say.

"Yeah. Years later he's giving an interview to a reporter, and he tells this story. The reporter says, 'So what happened?' W.C. says, 'I grew up and earned far more money than I ever dreamed I could earn. And I thought back to that promise I'd made all those years ago, about all those poor kids and the magic of the circus and how if I didn't make it possible for them to go, they'd never see it. And then I thought, "Screw 'em."'"

PART IV

LIFE AMONG THE HUMANS

CHAPTER 25

Tuna Helper and Jesus

Everywhere I turn I see people wanting to be leaders. There's the usual collection of Christian leadership jokers with their herds of humming zombies. And if a person loves the wisdom of women's basketball coaches and retired executives, there are Christian leadership conferences to attend nearly every weekend. It would be like following the Grateful Dead, and about as useful. Though to be fair, Deadheads aren't claiming to lead a brave new world, which gives them much greater credibility and probably makes them the better source for guidance. Celebrities talk about "using their celebrity" to influence culture. In some churches, the key is to be the "vision-caster" or the cultish personality around which the congregation can grow like barnacles on a scuttled ship. In other churches, it's apostle-this and prophet-that, and suddenly the television preachers all decided to call themselves Bishop-whatever and started wearing these nutty, pin-striped Nehru jackets with epaulets and aiguillettes looping their shoulders to indicate some vaguely military leadership post. Something about fashion and authority, they say, but I think the military touch has more to do with downplaying the hair helmets. Everywhere, everywhere, it's all chiefs and no braves. No bravery at all. Everyone on ship's got a megaphone and they're all yelling "stroke," but nobody's at the oars. And at long last, after so much yelling and jockeying for insight, I wonder how many people really have a sense of what we're supposed to be doing with the lives we've been given, anyway. I have to wonder where we're all being led, or to what end.

Of course, who'd want to row when there is so much glory in yelling? Who would want simply to live and labor and be present in an ordinary day, when the future promises to be so pain-free and sunny? Who'd want to be stuck doing work when there are so many lunches to share and navels ready to be gazed upon? Not me.

That's pretty much what brought things to an end for me at Five Points Christian Church. Pastor Arrington had no problem with my attending a different church on Sundays, so long as I was on time during the week, but I was running out of enthusiasm for the job and for the tensions there, and I wasn't being a very good employee anymore. I was ready to try something new. Mostly, I left because it was too hard being there, too unimportant, too inefficient, too low-profile, and playing the role of outsider was wearing thin. It made me a poor fit for the simple work the church needed me to do.

We decided together that I would move on — but if we hadn't decided it together, Pastor Arrington would have decided it for me. I knew it was coming, and I'd already found something else.

I was reading a book by Henri Nouwen, the Harvard professor who left his job to work and live with the developmentally delayed people of the L'Arche community of Daybreak in Canada, and I wanted to have a similar story to Nouwen's, where I was this super genius who was able to talk about how much he'd learned from the people who functioned so far beneath him. It sounded noble. Heroic, even.

Besides, the work at the place that wanted to hire me for this wouldn't be hard: just make my way through the apartment complex to the four units rented by seven men with varying sorts of developmental issues to wake them, get them fed, send some off to work, entertain the others, make sure they get their medications, cook lunch for some and dinner for nearly all, and hang out with them. And sleep in the second bedroom-turned-office-and-staff-smoking-den in one of the apartments. And the job was only Sunday through Tuesday evening. Perfect. Sign me up.

I told Pastor Arrington about my plan, and we agreed that the fit wasn't working as it had and wished each other well. I still feel conflicted inside, but I don't know what to do with that, so I focus on my relief about being done with the light rail and that bus route and on to new and more erudite things.

Being Henri Nouwen isn't quite what I expected. I thought I was going to enter a world where I would be this kindly fellow working with people who were naively friendly and honest and happy, with crisp edges regarding the things they could or could not do on their own.

Wrong.

Like the rest of the very best evangelicals, I want to be a leader, a difference-maker. You know, a left-brained, principle-driven hero with a closet full of Dockers. And I'm chafing that my arrival hasn't completely changed the lives of the men here. They lie and complain, a lot. And it feels lousy when Tim, the forty-year-old autistic guy I've spent hours with for weeks, freaks out if I happen to touch him. It's insulting — he should be playing by my rules of courtesy.

And there are no clear boundaries regarding what the guys are able to do, nor is there necessarily any progress. One day things go well, and the next the skill is lost.

William cleans bathrooms at a hotel near the old airport, and it means the world to him; but sometimes he drinks too much of the free Pepsi at the bar, and I get a call about how he's had diarrhea in his pants, and I need to drop everything and go take care of that. He feels awful, but he doesn't really get the whole cause-and-effect thing; and the people who work at the hotel are pretty much the sort of people who would encourage an overweight thirty-six-year-old with Down's syndrome to drink caffeine until he messed his pants.

William's roommate is Jimmy, who has Down's and is in his fifties. We think he's also developing Alzheimer's. Sometimes he gets so frustrated that I'll hear him upstairs from the office throwing things and yelling in his room. He has a hard time gauging how high to shave his sideburns, and how evenly, so right now he has none, and on the left side there is an extra channel cut in his hair about an inch higher than the top of his temple. When I take him out in public I wonder if people think I'm the monster who would cut a retarded man's hair that way. Neither William nor Jimmy understands why they're on diets, and both of them will steal food and eat until they get sick if they can.

Roommates Sam and Henry — I call them Sam Love and Henry Love — watch *Dukes of Hazzard* three times a day and know the lyrics to the theme song by heart. They both wear their cowboy hats whenever the show is on. Most of the time they're both great, but sometimes Sam will go into this compulsive mode and use his baseball card collection to build a card house one story high from the front door all the way through the apartment to the back, and when he does this Henry will sometimes end up trapped in his room because he doesn't want Sam to yell at him for messing up the cards.

In the middle of the night, Henry will call over to the office, crying because he can't get to the bathroom and doesn't know what to do.

Autistic Tim's roommate, Nick, is in his sixties, mutters non-sensically, and his osteoporosis has forced him to use a walker. Tim and Nick have a nameless cat to which I'm very allergic, so I pretty much only spend as much time at their place as is required to prepare their food or make sure they've taken their pills and brushed their teeth. And finally there is Hungarian Vince, whose second-biggest disability is that he doesn't quite look retarded. His dark, googly staring eyes, thick glasses, lopsided moustache, and often-twisted pants mostly make him look just creepy. People often greet him as though they expect a normal response from a merely unfortunate victim of a lousy pick in the cosmetic lottery. And sometimes his first sentence is lucid and clear enough that people don't see there are only fifty-four IQ horsepower working under the hood. By Vince's second sentence, most people understand. The dynamic has been painful in Vince's life because unlike the other guys in the program, Vince has seen the expression on the face of every person who has suddenly recognized that he is not like them.

I'm sitting at Vince's dining room table as we're trying, again, to make Tuna Helper. We chose Tuna Helper because he likes the taste and because there is nothing that will hurt him if it's undercooked. The words of the recipe on the box confuse him, so whenever we buy the stuff, I take a black marker and mark out everything but the pictures. Then together we find the measuring cups and the different ingredients. I've permanently marked the cups so he will know how far to fill them. I've marked the kitchen timer and the stove dial. We've made Tuna Helper together once a week for two months now. He has still never been able to do it without my intervention, but I'm determined that he will have this one victory.

Which reminds me about the whole leaders everywhere thing. The rewards in this job are just about nil. If, after months of working at it, Vince makes his own Tuna Helper, it's his victory. Sure, I will have played a part in teaching him, but I have to admit that teaching one retarded Hungarian to make Tuna Helper one time (I don't even begin to believe this will become a lasting skill) is not exactly what I was hoping to read about on my tombstone. I want my efforts, and my life's work, and my life, to pile up higher than that, to be seen from further away than that. I want to be a chief, not just a brave. And the pain of not getting that, the pain of having a job and life description that bears the prefix of "I'm just a . . . ," chafes a bit, especially when I think about how it all sounds back home. Thank goodness I'm arrogant jerk enough to turn that pain into a nice dose of elitism so I can throw stones rather than deal with living a humble life. I can look at those visionary leaders, those people whose words bring applause, and those pastors dressed like Austin Powers on parade, and I can say that all of their work is a reflection of their own need and greed because it all brings them a reward for their leadership. Mine brings me $6.25/hr plus half of the worst Tuna Helper in the world. I must be noble, right? Hey, maybe that nobility is impressive and worth following . . . just like I followed Nouwen.

Vince ends up needing my help with the Tuna Helper — I let him put in one extra cup of water, but when he's about to put in a second extra I know my dinner will be ruined and I step in. We're still left with Tuna Helper stew, but we eat it. With frozen corn and store-brand cola.

"Good job on this, Vince," I tell him as we slurp.

"Thanks," he says, looking up and staring.

And then he keeps staring.

"What?" I ask. The whole staff has been working with him to break the Hypnoto routine.

He smiles a goofy grin, the kind a person makes when they're waiting for the punch line they know is coming. With Vince, it just looks that way.

"Hey," he says.

"Yes, Vince."

"With God." I've been taking him to church with me for several weeks now.

"Yes?"

"What does God do at night when everybody's sleeping?"

Vince can't make sense of the picture drawings on a box of Tuna Helper; he's not going to get the whole Copernican thing. What did Denver Seminary teach me about this question in the Integrated Theology class?

"Well, Vince, at night God holds your heart, like this." I lay one hand palm up, and rest my other hand over it like I'm holding his heart. "And he squeezes it, like this. And each time he squeezes it, he says, 'I love you, Vince.'"

He stares at me, grinning like he's waiting for the punch line.

"Huh," he says. And then he goes back to his Tuna Helper.

Man, that was such a good answer too. It's like pearls thrown to swine around here. I'm a bright guy with some seasoned understanding about God and matters of great import. I could be out changing the world. I could be doing public relations for Habitat for Humanity. I could speak to a wide audience about life's seminal issues. Could I at least get a follow-up question? The rest of the important leaders at least get a follow-up question. Or an email telling them how well they did. Or a pat on the back or a "Pastor, your words changed my life" or something. I get "huh" from Hungarian Vince. Great.

———

Speaking of seminal issues, a brief word about Flora, the staff person with the overnight shift before mine. She's twenty-nine, with shiny black hair and a body that makes me ache the way a big steak makes me want to take a bite. She's totally sarcastic, and we joke rough. She smokes in a way that reminds me of the cashiers in the break room at the grocery store back home when I was in high school — all redneck with chips on their shoulders. She's married, but it sounds like they fight a lot, and mostly get along when they go out drinking. She grew up going to church and frequently asks questions about God and faith, but she also loves to make fun of my prudishness, all of which comes from her poking at stereotypes she accuses me of representing.

She knows I'm attracted to her and mercilessly toys with that fact. Company policy is that we're supposed to wash the sheets on the bed in the office at the end of our shift, but she usually doesn't. I think she knows that I can smell her on the pillow and that it torments me. When I'm feeling clean and strong, I wash the sheets during the hours our shifts overlap, to make a point. Other times I leave them and smell her in the moonlight, imagining her emerging from the bathroom and climbing into the bed with me. Her husband is a high-dollar salesman with a dark complexion and a cold heart. I picture how she would gladly trade for a soft, poor, blond guy with a giant heart and a pent-up need for love. Nothing will or would ever happen between us, and I only think of her when I'm here — it's certainly not a relationship or an obsession, but I can't stop myself from playing the game. At least not for long.

And I think about how much of my life is really just a clumsy acting out of some nutball fantasy that only makes sense in the middle of the night. It's bad enough starting off working from the nice guy angle because the pure physical attractiveness thing just isn't there; but add the extra warping pressure of this Christian subculture thing, and all of my own zealousness to be pure (a zeal, I confess, that is much more active in the moments when temptation or opportunity are not present), and I'm quickly becoming a tragic loss.

I know it's weird, but I think my approach to, and relationship with, women looks an awful lot like the way the Church interacts with and looks for response from the world. It's clear the world constantly poses the question, "Am I pretty?" The Church shows up and offers clumsy, controlling, ultimately selfish praise and assurance that's really asking, "If I'm the one who tells you that you're pretty, will you find me impressive enough for a long enough time to believe me?" The world's ugly girls fall for it, and the pretty ones say, "Who the heck are you, freak?" At root, the Church and the world can only build idols for one another, and can't answer each other's real questions any better than a smile from me or a kiss from Flora could answer ours. There's only one voice that can speak to souls. That's good news, but it's terrifying and horribly lonely news first, and I have yet to figure out how to make it real.

And it's caused me to think more about leadership. Here's what I've come up with. Leadership is best measured by the communion it facilitates between the follower and the Father. The question is not how many people follow you, but how effectively they pass through you. Jesus says he is the way to the Father. Paul says, "Follow me as I follow Christ." Leadership is an usher's sweeping hand gesture, and the intention is to move a person beyond the leader. Leadership faces forward, to the Son and the Father. Real leadership is aware of who's following; but it doesn't walk backward like those guys with the orange flashlights who guide airplanes into their parking places on the tarmac, following a line or working from memory about where the destination lies. I guess it comes down to a question of whether you think God stays put, or if he's dynamic and moving.

I think this is a very difficult tension, especially for evangelicals who have determined the very most important thing is the seeking and saving of nonbelievers. I have this picture in my head of evangelicalism that takes place at a high school running track. We're all born lined up at the starting line, and a gun sounds. We don't know it's a race, though, so we just stand up. We mill about and talk to each other. People spread a blanket on the grass beside the track and pour some coffee. Why not? And someone, for whatever reason — be it the arrows on the track or the painted lanes or the 100-yard finish strip or curiosity or just wandering around — someone wanders across the 100-yard line. They realize the line was important. That's salvation.

And they look back and see all of the people hanging out drinking coffee or whatever, and they run back and start grabbing people by the elbow, exclaiming that we must all cross the 100-yard line. They try different tactics and get different results, but they always go back for more people, dragging them across the line. That pile of people who've been dragged across the line, sitting there pouring fresh coffee — that's the Church today.

And the people who are dragged across the line are happy. They're told they achieved the important point of life on the track, and they're given a time and they compare notes on what it was like completing the journey. And someone spreads a blanket on the grass at the 110-yard mark and someone else pours the coffee, and they cheer every time a new person is dragged across the line. Sometimes people who have crossed the line go and help the pastor drag more people across.

The crowd drinking coffee at the 110-yard mark make a noise that folks who have not yet crossed the line can hear. While it sounds pretty clear and sometimes pretty good to people at the 90-yard mark, people at the 20-yard hear only chaotic condemnation and gibberish. And, of course, that noise makes the pastors seem even less desirable to the 20-yard folks when the pastors arrive, panting and desperate and all too frustrated and secretly hoping to be able to take the advice of W.C. Fields and leave the 20-yarders where they are.

It's fun for pastors to hear the cheering as they cross back and forth over the finish line, though there is a frustration they feel that the coffee and doughnut crowd doesn't help more or doesn't cheer in unison. When the pastor thanks the crowd for their encouragement and yelling or their help, everyone gets a quick feeling that they're doing something really great.

This metaphor goes on and on. But the person I want to be is the one who looks at the bend in the track and wonders where it goes. I want to be the guy who sees that in our tendency to build idols and hiding places, we're simply not good at encouraging people to cross the 100-yard line without resorting to manipulation and Machiavellian rationalizations. Especially where souls are concerned, the ends do not justify the means.

I want to start to follow the lane markings because it seems like there must be some reason they're there. And maybe after a few yards I'll start to trot. Then jog. Then keep jogging. And when I get all the way around and I cross the starting line again and I'm a little winded and people look up at me from the 10-yard line and wonder what the heck I'm doing and where the heck I'm from, I'll just nod and say, "S'up?" and keep going. And when I cross the 100-yard mark again there will be people who are confused that I didn't get a new time, and they'll be offended that I don't stop to face backward and chant and cheer with them. And at about this time I'll start to feel a certain joy simply in the running, like maybe that's why the track was built. Like maybe that's what I was built to do. And I'll cross paths with people wandering the other direction on the backstretch and we'll nod at each other and say, "S'up?" and keep going.

I bet if I run, someone else will run. And if we run, others will run. Imagine what a relief that will be for the pastors who drag people across the line all day long. And it will be frustrating and humbling for pastors who have only gone as far as the 110-yard line because they will lose the cheering of the coffee crowd and will not be the stars. But they will discover a new joy. Pastors could choose to run, could face forward and just go, trusting the spiritual gravity of a leadership that is not about influence, but about facilitating communion between the follower and the Father. The Father who built the track.

If I can come to that point — the point where I give up the worldview that thinks the 100-yard line is the point and the end of the race — if I can learn to prize Jesus's commandment to love God above all else, and jettison the rest of the baubles that get in the way and promise me a false safety, then all of this confusion and hassle and pain will be worth it.

And if I'm wrong, there will always be more leadership conferences and louder versions of the same old stuff that will always sound like angry chaos to people at different places on the track.

I admit that this all sounds so good to me because I want to be a hero for choosing the simple way that nobody seems to cheer for. I want to tell myself that what I'm doing with people like Hungarian Vince will eventually be validated and will eventually make me a hero nobody saw coming. I want to do what God wants, but I want to feel important and I want to feel loved, and I want to have some control over those things. Does my sinful motivation make me wrong about the other stuff? I can't tell.

It was a long night. I pulled the unwashed pillowcase from beneath my head and threw it across the room, trying to keep thoughts of

Flora at bay. I began to pray, and soon I was past my temptation and well into the prayer. I've wanted to be used, to be a holy man, to see the face of God. And as I lay there, I felt like I was lying in blackness the way a stage is black, and a white spotlight began to creep toward me. It was God, and I knew that when the light touched me, I would be truly in his presence, and I would be known completely. The light was gentle but pure and crisp, friendly and inviting, there in part because I had invited it, drawing closer. It slid up the side of the bed, without threat, without hurry, coming steadily and with a boldness that would neither rush nor wait. The light folded over the corner of the mattress to the surface of the bed and kept easing toward me. When it was maybe two inches from my arm, I panicked. I stopped praying, and I wanted desperately to get out of that moment. I was terrified. I opened my eyes with a start and lay there, trembling. And then I began to cry. For my junk, yes, but mostly because after all of this time and all of these intentions to follow boldly, bravely, when the reality of him is upon me, I'm still absolutely scared to death of God. I'm not ready. I still want to control him, to make him my idol. I felt him refuse to remain merely an accessory to decorate the idol of myself. He refused to leave the worship directed toward me. I felt all of this sweep over me, and something inside of me broke. There, in the dark of the twin bed, was the loneliest I've ever been.

I don't know what time I finally drifted off.

The morning sun fills the room. I get up and throw the sheets in the washing machine, slip into the clothes I wore yesterday, and open the bedroom door to go check in with the guys in their apartments. Vince is eating cereal in front of the television, repeating a commercial slogan he saw during the Broncos game yesterday.

"Foster's. Australian for beer." He's really trying to get the accent. He shakes his head at how it sounds and takes another oversized scoop of flakes.

"Good morning, Vince," I say, walking past and opening the front door.

"Hey," he says.

I turn around.

He puts his spoon down in the bowl, and uses that hand to pat his chest.

"Been listening to my heart." He grins like he's waiting for the punch line.

I stop. I stare. I don't know what to say. I stammer something about that being great. I feel happy and shamed and confused about what to make of his comment and its ultimate meaning. Hungarian Vince is the first person I ever introduced to Jesus, my Lord whom I love and fear and who uses me in spite of myself.

CHAPTER 26

MUGGING THE TOOTH FAIRY

Moments when God crawls up the side of my bed in the form of a spotlight are rare. Instances where I encounter some evidence of my positive impact on the world happen about as frequently. And as with any moment of clarity, it is followed by conviction. In my ordinary, day-to-day world, I help Vince do his shopping and then steal his Pizza Rolls. Or I'll hang out with Sam Love and Henry Love watching television in their apartment longer than they'd prefer, browsing their kitchen. I don't know if there is anything more disgusting and virulent to the souls of other people than authority, especially authority self-conceived as love, living out its addictions at the expense of others. In my case, I don't want to be bothered to get up and steal their food, so I ask one of the guys to bring it to me. And I don't have the energy or desire to pack everyone into the car and head out for an adventure somewhere, like the mountains or a park, and will only do so when I get roped into it when one of the other staff people insists it would be a good idea.

I said it casually, but it hits me in waves now that I've put it out there: I steal food from retarded people who depend upon my honor and my professed dedication to their well-being. I am teaching them that this is how love treats them. I am teaching them that nothing is their own and that I may intrude upon their privacy whenever my ever-growing stomach experiences the urge. And William and Jimmy, the two men on diets, don't see me other than when I stop in for mandatory rounds for medications or that sort of thing. They don't have anything I want badly enough to climb the flight of stairs to their empty-cupboard apartment.

Most of the time I ignore this horror by keeping all of the rationalizing "yeah, buts" swirling around. Yeah, but:

I'm nicer to them than any of the other staff.

I take Vince to church with me, and sometimes take others.

I am making only six dollars an hour doing this job, and I have no car and I count on the grocery coupons that come as perks with my employment, while the men in the program actually have a surplus of both funds and food.

I am the guy who puts medicine in their ears.

I am the guy who once rested his hand in a cooling puddle of semen Henry Love had left on a blanket.

I am the guy who will take the whole crew out to the gourmet burger place.

I am the guy who took Sam and Henry Love to the country line-dancing bar even though they were dressed like cowboy clowns (or so I thought until we walked into the place, and I saw everyone else there). I bought them beer and we played pool. At one point, Henry shot the cue ball off of the table and it rolled across the room and under the next table. Sam went after it, but rather than going around the neighboring table, he crawled under it. The hotshot young man in the western shirt and Stetson with the date in tight acid-washed jeans with acid-washed bangs was horribly offended, and began to ridicule Sam. I'm the large man who walked over to the young man and said, "You two are dressed the same way. He's retarded. What's your excuse?" We returned to our game and I had fun eyeballing the young man the rest of the evening, joyfully aware that his being humiliated after mocking a retarded man wouldn't bode well for his chances of seeing his date's acid-washed undergarments.

I'm the guy who's here because he read Henri Nouwen, dang it.

It's all well and good that I have a Jesus sponge clamped onto my shell, and that I have some protection from the squid, but not everything in the world is a predator to me. There are a great many things — people — who are smaller than I am, and in my obsession with the squid and with my own defenses, I am willing to do harm and hide behind the rationalizations and selfish compulsions that I hold even closer to myself than I hold Jesus. How's that for being a creep? A coward and a bully, a manipulator and a fool — all at the same time.

Not that I'm actively aware of the trade I'm forcing. Not that I consciously think about how I charge my greedy, thieving behavior as an uninvited guest against my gentleness with the challenges of retarded men. It's more that I keep myself unaware of my own monstrosity by keeping a tally list of cute anecdotes or moments of praise from the guys. I think about how Jimmy loves to sit on the floor beside my easy chair in Vince's family room and stroke my arm saying I'm his friend. I think about William, who is barely verbal, singing "bright, bright sun-shiny day" along with the radio in the back seat on the way back to work after coming home to wipe the diarrhea from his body. I think about Vince lying in bed listening to his heart. I think about how God really does love Vince, and how he loves me too.

Of course I know better than to pay attention to my pulse and think about God's love in such immediate ways. I prefer a bit of distance. I'm much more likely to stop and notice the sunset on a Sunday evening and whisper some prayer like, "You never take a day off, do you?" I tend to appreciate him more as a peer.

I think people are impressed by the work I do and the way I live. I'm broke, and every Tuesday evening someone from my Bible study picks me up from work to drive me to whichever apartment we've chosen for the evening's study and flirtation. I regale the group with stories of living with the loving, demanding, challenging, least of these who I imply would be far worse off if it wasn't for me. I scoop praise from the group like a world-class melon baller, dragging my words and my eyes and my heart tweaks across each of them to extract my reward. I do the same thing over meals with people who want to meet me because some shared friend thought we'd like each other. I have become a master at the dance of godly caveat, of feigned vulnerability, carefully Teflon-coated and shined up. Sometimes I work to make someone I've just met cry at the stories I spin — that's a favorite response of mine. Sometimes I talk about the challenges and how God is showing me something "again," I say, so as not to be ranked as only learning this lesson for the first time and thus be found wanting. Deep down, but only way deep down, I know that I'm cashing in on these moments because I don't really believe God loves me or that his love for me is enough. It has everything to do with not being able to handle it when the light slides up the bed — everything to do with taking from Jesus without giving myself to him.

I craft my story carefully. I want the politely declined reward to be insistently thrust upon me — now in my humble posture, and later in heaven because I didn't quite cash it in fully here. As though I could fool God and man and myself and double up on the prize I did very little to earn in the first place. As a child I once pulled the coins from the glass of water the Tooth Fairy had filled without removing the tooth, and was thus rewarded two nights in a row. When I got away with that, I didn't know which was worse, the doubt I developed regarding the reality of a Tooth Fairy who could be so easily tricked, or the justice I was certain to eventually experience if indeed she did exist. Little has changed, I'm afraid.

And if the abusive choices I make to favor my addictions over the retarded men, my friends, and my friends' friends weren't enough, I turn the screws that much further with my family. They love me, and my mother in particular has determined to be my champion in all things. No matter what I say or do, she will find something to praise, and she will almost always offer her praise in the form of a comparison to her own value. She's an easy mark, and it kills me to think what I take from her every time I get the chance. Not only do I milk every good deed for all the praise I can get; not only do I trumpet every clever insight of my own or someone else's to my credit with my mother; not only do I use her protective fear to elicit additional care and concern; but also I turn every bit of what I'm doing into a fine-pointed weapon to pierce and condemn her for not doing likewise. She offers me praise by lowering herself, and I slam my heavy boot on her back and demand she drop further yet. Still I have the audacity to pray, to call myself a believer, to cite the Bible, and to claim that I am some sort of a positive presence in the lives around me. I believe what God says about me and my value. I know what I experience in prayer. I know that he is near, that he even lives within me, but there is such a disconnect. I simply cannot keep the realities of my behaviors, the extorted expenses of my addictions, in front of me at the same time as I speak of how I am fearfully and wonderfully made. I know that in the same night I can experience the failure of lurid fantasies concerning a married woman and also the immediate reality of a God whose love for me is greater than my ability to remain still and experience it. It is an exquisite torture, the evidence of heaven and hell mingled and foaming as ravenous fighting dogs within me. I can't tell for sure which fighting dog I'm rooting for, and I couldn't even begin to muster the courage to shoot the other.

Meanwhile, life with Vince and the gang continues. The Tuesday afternoon sun has warmed the steamy grass beside the steps to Vince's apartment, and we lie on it together, waiting for Skinny Robert to arrive to take me to Bible study. Vince is wearing gray slacks a size too big for him, cinched tight and lopsided under a very long belt. The tail of his purple silk dress shirt hangs out in back. His thick glasses look like the smudged observation window at the children's aquarium. He doesn't know the injustices I perpetuate in his world. He doesn't want me to go. He will miss me until I return next Sunday, and he will be sad when Robert arrives; but he will be proud to spot Robert first and to ask Robert how it's hanging.

Vince speaks Hungarian fluently, or at least as well as his elementary-level English. He loses his thought midstream pretty often, but for the most part he can carry on a conversation. When he calls his father, who lives about ten minutes away, they always speak Hungarian.

"Hey, Vince," I say. "Can you teach me some Hungarian?"

"I don't know."

"You speak it, right?"

"Yeah."

"Maybe you can teach me how to say something in Hungarian."

"I don't know."

"Okay, well, how do you say, 'Give me some money' in Hungarian?"

He stares blankly at me, waiting for the punch line. He is suddenly being tested, and he is uneasy.

"Try it this way. How would you say, 'Give me some money' to your dad?"

He furrows his brow and lunges toward me, yelling in a rough voice, "Give me some money!" Then, fearful that he's broken one of the rules of appropriate social behavior, he quickly rolls back to where he was lying and says, "Only joking."

"No, Vince. You know how when you talk to your dad you speak in a different language, the one I don't understand?"

"Yeah."

"That's Hungarian, right?"

"Yeah."

"If you were speaking in that language, how would you say, 'Give me some money'?"

His face shows that he is confused and is starting to feel as though he is failing me. He hates when he feels stupid. A bit of panic is creeping into his face. I should shift away from this line of questioning, but, come on, how hard is it to offer a simple phrase, after all? I push on, selfishly.

I make the hand gesture where I rub my thumb and forefinger together. I ask, "How do you say this in Hungarian?"

"*Adja meg az egyes penz!*" he says. Or at least it sounds something like that.

"Great job, Vince!" I exclaim. "*Aja mage es eggs pans?*"

He nods. Then a look comes over his face like the punch line is going to be bad. Then he begins to reach into his pocket to give me his money.

"No, Vince. I was just trying to say it like you did."

He stares at me, the look returning to happy punch line, but still not making complete sense.

"I don't want your money, Vince. You keep it, okay?"

"Okay."

I lie back down, breaking eye contact with him to let the moment cool. And suddenly I know what I will talk about at Bible study. We are, each of us, split into two worlds: the spiritual world where we pray and feel something of the eternal beauty of our creation; and the physical world where we are wet turds. I am capable of some kindness, but I am also capable of tremendous failures. Still, I have been created as an eternal being for whom God was pleased to die to be reconciled. I can pray and can experience something of the ecstatic, something of the eternal and ethereal. And I know somehow that truth could be translated into the physical reality of my daily, corporeal world. But somewhere this obvious thing, this obvious translation, has been lost to me. Call it the retardation of the Fall, perhaps.

It's obvious when I'm praying that I'm supposed to take what I encounter there and apply it to my everyday world. And in my everyday world it's obvious that a greater truth transcends what I experience and promises the hope of redemption. But for the life of me I cannot make the leap. I feel as though I'm failing — God, myself, the world, whatever — and a bit of panic begins to set in. I make clumsy, lunging attempts at a translation in the way I live, how I serve, how I think of or relate to God or the world, and then I see that they are clumsy, or wrong, or even punishable, and I recoil. I live on the grassy hill in the sun with a God I'd like to understand, whom I'd love to please and with whom I would love to converse and experience the world, whose company I miss when I don't feel him near me. It is torture that I cannot quite comprehend what it all means, or what he's after.

Jesus is the hand gesture. Jesus makes sense to the physical side of me and to the spiritual. Vince can say Jesus's name in English or Hungarian, but only if you point to the crucifix and ask who hangs upon it. Vince will fail if you start in one language and ask for the translation. I cannot start with prayer and translate the Truth to the world. I cannot start with the world and extrapolate sublime Truth. I must always fall back to the person of Jesus, without all of the language on one side of the divide or the other. So long as I do that — work from the independent reality of Jesus instead of the lexicon of either of my languages — I turn out to be less retarded than I thought. And God will applaud my success. Even if I don't understand that all he was trying to get me to see is that he loves me and wants me completely, and instead I try to empty my pockets before him.

And in Bible study people will think I am insightful and am developing this great relationship with the people I'm serving. Later, I will find an even richer way of talking about all of this with friends of friends. Then I will call home, and I will make my mother feel as though she is nothing compared to me, and I will hang up feeling the cold comfort of a sacrificial compliment whose value I'm too big a monster to appreciate. And then I will pray and God will start again at trying to help me see the hand gesture and what that gesture must ultimately, even if fleetingly, mean about my life.

CHAPTER 27

FAITH SAILS UNRAVELING

"Wow, you really got sunburned today," the dockmaster says to me as he ferries Skinny Robert and me from Robert's sailboat to shore. The lake is encircled by mountains and is one of my favorite places.

"That's nothing," Robert says. "See how swollen he is? He's usually my size."

I start to smile, but my face is too tight and too burnt. I know better than to punch him either — he'd just slap me and leave me howling. The dockmaster laughs politely and drops us at the beach.

It's been a great day, just the two of us out on *Zuzu's Petals*, whipping up and down the lake with its Rocky Mountain shores. I spent most of the afternoon sitting on the bow, my feet dangling on the tops of the waves, enjoying the Bob Marley music Robert was playing in the stern. There is room for two to sleep comfortably below deck, which is our plan for after dinner and an aloe vera hunt in town.

The dockmaster is gone by the time we return to the lake. We swim out to the boat. Nobody else is around. We change into our spare clothes and break out the cigars. Robert has never smoked one before.

"No, like this," I say.

He coughs. He spits. He tries again a couple of times, but when it burns out he doesn't relight it.

"David and Danielle are pregnant," I say.

"Really? Cool for them."

"Yeah. It is."

I smoke some more. Minutes pass, the moon glazing the night as the breeze brushes the rigging against the mast and turns the boat gently around its bow-end mooring.

"You know, Robert, in the past month the only human affection I've had has been a couple of hugs from Danielle."

"Been there."

"They say that babies who aren't held become sociopaths and serial killers."

"And Starbucks baristas."

"I feel like bad things are happening to me, like I'm starving from lack of contact."

"Keep talking like this and you'll sleep up here," he says.

"I feel like my dreams are dying."

"What do you mean?"

"I used to dream about the details of my future. A thousand different romantic ways to propose. A million gentle things I wanted to whisper to my wife. I pictured my daughter riding her pink bike with glittering tassels past me yelling, 'Look, Daddy.' I dreamed of teaching my son to cook an omelet, and making a complete mess. I saw myself surrounded by noise and color and action and needs and crying and being the dad who could shoulder it all, who could make it all better. And who would be a wizard on the backyard barbecue. I dreamed of catching my wife looking at me lovingly, and of her simply kissing me and returning to whatever she was doing when I asked why she was staring at me."

"Mmm."

"I remember my dad's thirtieth birthday. I was six, and my brothers were four and two. My dad was married when he was twenty-three and was finished having children by the time he was twenty-eight. I'm twenty-five now, and I'm way behind schedule. I don't even see any prospects. I feel like I'm freezing to death, like the way people lose their fingers and toes first, and then the cold creeps nearer and nearer to their cores, and eventually they're found stripped naked with some grotesque grimace on their face because — in the midst of the freezing — they suddenly felt hot and went running out into the snow. I already feel the fingertip dreams like my little girl and her bike with tassels, or even the little girl herself, freezing and breaking off, lost forever."

I puff on my cigar. A few seconds pass.

"Who said you're supposed to be on the same schedule as your dad?" Robert asks. "And after everything you've said about Betsy, can you imagine what your world would be like if you had married her?"

"Yeah, I guess I dodged the bullet there. And I know I'm grieving the loss of an unreal life plan, but that doesn't make any difference; it still feels the way it feels."

"I understand. I feel a big chunk of that every time I take Daniel back to his mother at the end of a weekend at my place. It wasn't supposed to be like this."

"So why is it, Robert?"

"The Fall, I guess. Sin and death spilled everywhere."

"I know that answer too. Does it make sense to you?"

"No," he admits. "I can tell it's true, but in terms of comfort it feels more like a wet blanket than a warm embrace."

"Stupid Adam," I say.

"Stupid Eve," he adds.

"Morons."

"Idiots."

"I'd have done the same thing."

"We all would have."

"Hey, relight your cigar."

"Nah. It's not my thing." He throws it into the water. We fall to silence, and I wonder how bad it is to call Adam, the first man created by God, a moron.

"I'm so sunburned I can feel the heat coming off my body."

"You smell like my grandma. The aloe, not the cigar. She says cigars don't go as well with her vodka as a pipe does."

I grin in the dark. "If you keep talking about how I smell like your grandma, you can be the one to sleep up here," I say.

A minute passes, the end of my cigar glows orange, and I practice blowing smoke rings.

"Why do you do it, then?" Robert asks.

"Do what?"

"Put so much energy into your deal with God?"

"For the fame and fortune," I say.

"No, really. Why?"

"I guess because I don't know what else to do. I don't know how I'd stop. I have so much bet in the pot that I can't fold my hand now. I need God to have something he wants me to do, some role to play."

"But that doesn't mean you have to build your whole world around doing the stuff," Robert says.

"I want to be as defined by him as I can be."

"Sometimes it just seems like you overpay. Sometimes it seems like you choose to overpay."

"You're right. I do." I don't know what else to say. "It's something I do because I want to earn God's love because I can't just let it happen without taking him for granted, or maybe I'd hate him if he loved me for no reason. I don't know for sure yet — and I don't know why I'm afraid to really figure it out."

"So you're sort of in a holding pattern?"

"Maybe. I feel like he's showing me stuff — maybe the same stuff over and over until I get it. I haven't gotten it yet, though, so yeah, I guess I'm in a holding pattern as a Jesus freak. I know that what's holding me back is plain old fear and pride, but I don't know what else to try to let go. So I just keep trying, and it seems like all that's happening is that I'm getting weirder and weirder. Especially in the eyes of my family."

"Nobody's family understands them."

"You're right. Of course, you're right. I'm just feeling melancholy. And your question about why I do this is a good one. Maybe it's partly to keep distance from people."

"Like Rachel, if she has an opening among the *homme du jour?*" he asks.

"Yeah, maybe especially her. I could sure go for a hug from her."

"It would be squishy in all the right ways."

"I don't know how many times the word 'boundaries' has come up when I talk to people about her."

"Speaking of which, it's time for me to get to sleep or we'll be up all night. You still won't have any boundaries tomorrow, and we can talk about it then."

"Alright. I'm going to sit up here for a while."

"Sleep well. I'll most likely kill you in the morning," he quotes from a favorite movie and then disappears into the cabin.

I work my way back up to the bow and hang my feet over the edge like I did this afternoon. I really don't know why I'm doing all of this with God, and I can tell that my behavior is more erratic because I can't express why I'm doing any of it. I talk about my motivation being to know as clearly as possible in this life that from which I have been separated. I want to know as much of God as I can, because I'm living for the moment of my death. I dream of that moment, of the moment I first see Jesus, and I want it to feel like I've only barely been removed from him, and all I have to do is lean forward into an embrace. An embrace. How sweet that sounds to me tonight. And his, no less. I want to know exactly how to respond, because I want to have spent my life in his company. I don't want to be uncertain about whether to bow or hide or weep or run or leap into his arms or what. I want to press into the ever-shrinking gap between us, to savor the distance, to feel it, to yearn against it, and then one day to melt through it and into his arms in the moment of my last breath.

I think it's a beautiful goal. The rub is that it's hard to engage with life itself when life is pretty much only an object lesson or a testing ground or a barrier that I'm ultimately interested in eliminating.

The moon rests on the water's horizon, and the path of white reflected light pours itself to me. For a long time I quietly sing and pray. I think about the time when I felt like Jesus and I were hanging out for the day, and how when I stopped to get gas I told him, "You know how much money I have in my pocket — you decide when to stop the gas pump." The pump stopped at exactly $11. I reached into my pocket and found a ten and a one-dollar bill. I laughed and said, "Okay, you know how much change is in there too. I'll top this off, and you stop it when I get to the last penny." I didn't have any other form of payment on me. I began to top the tank off. Eighty-two cents later the Jeep would take no more. I fished around in my pocket and found exactly eighty-two cents. It was a delightful moment, a moment when this Jesus with whom I'd been spending the day played a game with me and I knew he was right there.

That's the Jesus, and those are the moments, that delight me and make me long for the embrace that will come when the veil between this place and the next is removed. This is the Jesus who inspires me to be weird, even if I am clumsy and even if I tend to overpay. Even if people find me too confusing to be desirable as a result. I thank Jesus that I know him.

And then I suddenly feel a tiny invitation in my gut to step out onto the water. I know that if I step out, it will hold, just as it did for Peter. I sit transfixed, the moment pregnant with the magic of "what if." The feeling urges me to move, pleads with me to simply step out onto the water. I feel my muscles begging to slide off the edge of the boat. And then I think about how Peter began to sink, and I think about something else, and then I think about something else, and then the moment is gone, and I find myself sucked back into my brain once again. I don't move.

What did I have to lose? There was no prospect of shame if I had stepped onto the water and fallen in. It would not have surprised Robert if I had tried. And there was an incredible experience to gain if it had worked. What if the water had held? What if? What would I do with that fact? How much would that upset my understanding of the world, and how wondrously so? But once again I'm shown that I simply do not believe the way I say I believe.

Why is it so much easier to venture out away from a career and into ministry and poverty than it is to risk simply getting wet? Am I that tied to my control and my brain? Is this all just a game, where I am willing to trust what I can argue but not what I can only feel and act upon? Have I changed that much since I felt the huge leap of moving out here just because I had a hunch? Am I worried that God won't come through? Am I working to protect my fragile faith, worried that if the water doesn't hold I won't step out later with other things?

Maybe. Probably. Yes.

When I was at Turnaround, my mom's friend Melinda had cancer, and I prayed and told my mom I thought God wanted to heal the cancer, but wanted it to be something that we all contributed to. Not a surprising strategy given the "tremendous man of God" setting and personal place I was in at the time. I told her I thought we should pray and do different sorts of fasts for her. Mom gave up Diet Coke, and others gave up different things, and every time they wanted the things from which they were fasting, they would pray for Melinda. An entire community grew around her.

Once when I was home I went to her house to meet her. Mom had told her a great deal about me. She was desperate. As we sat by the sunny window of her Victorian living room, she asked me what I thought she should do. She was overwhelmed with fear and sadness.

I told her to sing.

I felt like an idiot, a little idiot child with no decorum regarding the gravity of her situation for saying it, but I told her she should sing. I told her there was still much to celebrate, no matter what happened, and that she should sing. Tears came to her lashless eyes and rolled down her sallow cheeks. She asked me if I knew she was from a family of musicians, and that her mother had sung with the Metropolitan Opera. It was the perfect answer, and it melted her. I had her sign my journal, as I have had each of the retarded men do since, to pray for her. I still believed that she would be healed, and not just in some "it brought the family together and she died in peace" sort of way. I still believed that her sickness would be removed and that she would show up at church or the movies.

But she died about six weeks after I told her to sing. And that was the last time I've ever believed that a miracle has been promised to me, and it was the last time I ever let someone else see that I had even so much as a hunch that something special could happen. I felt like I had abused my mother and her friends, and Melinda too, for that matter. I'd been wrong, and I'd been wrong while claiming to speak for God. I was selling the wrong-sized Jesus, a sponge that would not cover us all, and the squid ate its fill. I was ashamed of my advice. I was ashamed of God's behavior. I was ashamed that I'd not been hearing the right voice somehow. I'd believed him, and they'd believed me, and we'd all been duped. I didn't have a place for that. I was already well aware that I was living this quixotic life, this forever chasing after the next grand endeavor, and I knew that the dragons usually turned out to be windmills in my own world, and that was okay because in my own world I was after the adventure and the prospect that one day, just one day, the dragon would be real and I would know my identity as a gallant charging knight. But I had no sense of the caveat about my tendency to trust illusions when I told my mother to believe that her friend would not die of an emaciating cancer. I had no place for that, and my childlike faith, the romantic faith that believed, was made to feel like a fool. So I put it neatly away, folded respectfully but tucked away with the other relics of childhood and childish dreams, like the Batman cap or the magic flying blanket.

I knew that something had broken in me when Melinda died, but I still assumed that when I was alone, sitting for an hour on the bow of a friend's boat in the moonlight, and I felt as though Jesus was inviting me out onto the water, I would trust enough to risk it. I was wrong.

CHAPTER 28

AIDAN

Today is the day Danielle will have her first child. Two nights ago I joined them for a dinner of spicy Chinese food because someone had told her that spicy food sometimes induces labor. I arrive at the hospital in shorts and an untucked light blue shirt, Tevas on my feet and a cooler on my shoulder. In it are green grapes, shrimp, cheese, crackers, drinks, and other assorted party snacks.

Danielle's parents are in the room with the happy couple when I arrive, and together we enjoy the sun and the sound of the mother and child heartbeat monitors. Quiet music is playing, most notably Rich Mullins' "Let Mercy Lead," a song sung to a child named Aidan, which is what David and Danielle have decided to name their son. David is nearly twitching with excitement, and Danielle has felt great ever since the spinal block. We keep replaying the Aidan song, and David says he wants it to be playing when his son arrives. Danielle's mother, Sue, glows in the striped sunlight pouring through the window blinds. Randy, Danielle's father, says Sue looks ready to be a grandma, rolling back and forth in the blond wooden rocking chair. The expectant grandmother nearly explodes with joy at the thought. Danielle says not to eat all of the food; she wants some later.

And then it is time for Randy and Sue and me to leave the room for the delivery. We stand in the hallway outside the room, and we listen to the activity inside. We joke about whatever comes to mind. The sounds inside the room escalate, and then we hear the cry of a baby. I congratulate Randy, and he congratulates me on becoming an honorary uncle. Randy hugs Sue, and then he notices that she is looking out of the corner of her eye as though she is listening carefully to what's happening inside the room.

"What?" Randy asks.

"He only cried one time," Sue answers.

We all pause, straining our ears. It's the first time the possibility of things not going perfectly seems to have occurred to Randy. I know it's the first time I've considered it.

Inside we hear Danielle. "What? What's wrong?"

There is motion inside the room. The door flies open and a nurse runs down the hallway.

"What's going on?" Danielle has not given in to her fear, but it's clearly building within her.

We hear David speaking to her in low tones.

Sue's hand rises to her mouth, and her eyes go red and wet. Aidan still has not made another sound.

The three of us step across the hallway to look back through the open doorway without blocking it. There is a curtain drawn between us and Danielle. Sue pushes into Randy's chest.

We hear something about the NICU, and we hear the locks being flipped on the wheels of a cart, and then the cart with Aidan under its plastic bubble passes through the door and by us. David is following closely, pushing the curtain aside. Danielle is covered in sheets and baby blue hospital gown. Her eyes are locked on David, who turns back to her and stops. A fierce promise transpires in their gaze, and David runs to catch up with the nurses and his newborn son. Danielle sees her mother. Time stops. A nurse closes the door.

David is gone a very long time. When the doctors wrap up with Danielle, Sue goes into the room. I stay with Randy in the waiting area. We pace and wander around some from time to time, drinking decaf. At one point two nurses heading from the NICU see us, but not until one of them says, "But it sure doesn't look good." Her face freezes, both Randy and I are transfixed, and then she decides to pretend that she wasn't talking about Aidan as she and her coworker pass us.

I promised to call back to Zionsville and tell family friends how things went. I try my mother, but she's not home. David's mother and her husband are in Maine, and I wouldn't dare be the one to call them anyway. I try the church but get voicemail. I dial a friend of David's mother, and she answers. I hadn't realized just how unprepared I was to say anything yet. As soon as the thought about my words comes to me, I collapse into tears in the small phone nook.

"Something's wrong," I say.

"Oh, my God." Betty gasps. "How wrong?"

"It doesn't — "

"What?"

"He only cried once. He's alive, but we don't know what's happening."

"Oh, no. Oh, Danielle."

I'm a wreck.

"What do you know?" Betty's voice pushes through my trembling groans.

"Nothing," I choke out. "I heard a nurse say it didn't look good. He's not going to make it." I don't know this, but the horror of it tackles me and I say it.

"Oh, God. I'll start calling people and we'll start praying. Has anyone called Don and Sue in Maine?"

"I don't know. I think they were getting a flight today, anyway, but I don't know if they've been told anything yet."

Hours later David and Danielle are alone in her room, and friends and family gather in hushed tremor in the waiting area. The diagnosis is hypoplastic left heart syndrome. There is something wrong with how the blood is pumping and how much oxygen is getting to the blood. When Danielle is wheeled to the NICU, or when David is with Aidan, the machine providing him oxygen doesn't have to work as hard. Yet when the physicians touch him, Aidan's body needs 20 percent more help from the machines. Comfort? Terror? Why does this happen? We're told that surgery is going to be likely.

A day passes.

And a second. Still we wait together, stunned, wanting to hope, holding back grief, not wanting to lose faith, not wanting to jinx the process.

On the third day Aidan is wheeled into the operating room, still having shown no improvement. Still having never made a second sound. The operation will involve snaking an instrument through an artery in his thigh all the way to his heart. There is an imbalance of pressures in his heart. There will be massive amounts of anti-coagulant used to keep his blood from clotting too quickly, but the same drug will also make the surgery extremely dangerous. We wonder how much difference the altitude pressure will make. David and Danielle come and go. Friends from seminary wait with the parents. A thousand understood theological answers, and nothing to say about what is happening. We pray. We pray a lot.

We hear Danielle's response to the news that the surgery did not go well, and that Aidan died on the table. Fierce embraces are exchanged. We weep and weep for what seems like hours. I hug Danielle and find myself apologizing for the whisker rub my beard delivers. Through horrible tears we find ourselves laughing. There is simply too much to feel it all. David and Danielle go to be with Aidan. He was cut open during the surgery, and when he did not survive, there was little reason to close the incisions well. With all of the anti-coagulant in his body, the blood soaks through towel after towel. David holds his son until his shirt is drenched with the baby's blood.

Aidan is cremated. I go with David to pick up the ashes. It is my first time holding the boy. Now the hard part begins for David and Danielle, and in some ways, for all of us.

CHAPTER 29

Why God Made Moms

Mom came out for the funeral, where Aidan's song was played. Despite everything, it's been a great week for me with her, and now I'm watching her airplane taxi away from the gate. I'm going to feel alone again in a few minutes, but not yet.

I'm glad my mom was here for such an emotion-packed week. Some older people questioned the choice to have a funeral for a baby who died after only three days of life. Other people said things like how at least the grieving process wouldn't be as hard because David and Danielle never really knew Aidan. Other people seemed to keep track and have strong opinions about how much time is appropriate to dedicate to mourning. It was horror on top of horror for Danielle, who has not only been grieving the loss of her child, but also has had to fight for permission to do so. She's had to face the obnoxious question: Are you still a mother after your child dies?

The answer is most certainly yes.

Every mother knows grief. Regret, fear, failures, changes in motherly roles. All of these make a very particular grief truly known only by mothers, and it is experienced in miscarriages, funerals for children, and even in the celebration of a continuing and decent enough relationship with children who have long since outgrown their mothers' laps. It also seems that, like Danielle, most mothers are challenged regarding the value of their desires to be mothers, challenged for the practicality of their love itself, and eventually challenged to find something else to drop neatly into the space left achingly void in their hearts when the child moves along — the space that is only truly matched by the individual children who created those spaces in her heart in the first place.

My mother is trying to figure out what's next for her. My dad will be retiring soon, early, and he knows what's next for him. A growing passion for Romania has mystified us all, but he has already repeatedly visited a tiny village to work with an orphanage and church there. Mom is feeling the pressure to find her own next thing. We assume grandchildren will be coming at some point, but she feels like she's supposed to have a ministry or job passion, something she does outside of the home. In the past she has talked about children's books.

As we discuss our respective desires to be used, to have a mission in life, it strikes me that we're more alike than I'd thought for a long time. Maybe we're not the only ones. Both my mother and I are determined to point to something outside of ourselves to demonstrate our worth and our utility. The crab shell must be covered, well and completely, beautifully and wisely, by a collection of things or by the sponge of Jesus held desperately by hopelessly inadequate hind legs, or we will have no one to blame but ourselves when the squid brings the pain. We want to be important enough to be loved, both of us.

Strangely, somewhere both my mother and I have come to believe worth and utility are the same thing. But they are not. There is a great difference between being worthless and being useless, and there is a great difference between the things that make us useful and the true measure of our worth. One is what we do, and the other is what we are. One is developed and grown, and the other is full and unchanging from the moment of our conception.

But it's hard to build an economy on worth. It's hard to move a society forward, given our dedication to Darwin's rules of merit-based living, with inherent personal value. Grades don't measure intrinsic importance.

And it does come down to importance, because in measuring importance we find some way of measuring our relative position to our need for the God we're all desperate not to need. We're certainly here to do work, and utility is an important thing, and there are absolutely a great many valid and critical reasons why we build such potent structures of reward and punishment around utility and counter-productivity. The trap is that for all of our obsessions regarding our status on the scales of utility, none of it means squat about what we're really worth.

Everyone knows this. I know this, and my mom knows it too. God loves me. Good. I know. It's good news, warm and fuzzy and sweet sounding. It's worthy information, but it's totally useless information because it sure as heck isn't going to help me get the job if I put it on my resume. The phone company won't take my intrinsic value in lieu of payment for my delinquent bill. No wonder it's so hard to pay attention to. No wonder I can hear about God loving me, and still have this incredible need to go prove that his love has been rewarded, and that by my efforts some fraction of his mercy has been preserved for use on someone else. No wonder I can conceive of being useful enough to be worth something more than was already worth grieving from the first moment of my existence. No wonder I don't know wonder.

As the plane lifts off and I brace for the return of feeling alone, I think God grins about the ironic coolness of Truth, and about what good news exists in the fact that we have it all backward.

I mean, what could be more truly useful than the useless truth about my worth? What could be more helpful to me as I live in a fallen world than to finally get that I am loved beyond the reasons to love me, and that I am worth more than the love I earn? What could be more practical knowledge than to know, in a way that means I know it as though it is absolute fact, that however my other endeavors may go, however many dragons turn out to be windmills and however many times the water doesn't hold beneath my feet and however many times the people for whom I pray still die, that however any of these things go, there is nothing to be gained or lost regarding my ultimate position in the universe? What could be more practical wisdom in the world than the wisdom that would free people to live and love for the sake of loving and living, not because they were looking for a reflection of themselves by which they could measure their own cosmic height? What could be better, more practical, and helpful knowledge to the world than for us to know that we were all born already tall enough for this ride?

And as soon as I think it, I lose it again. As soon as it becomes clear, it slips from me. I think that's because as soon as I think it, as soon as it becomes clear, I want to translate it into action, and as soon as I do that I hit the wall of translation that my soul, and creation, is flatly unable to overcome.

That's what mothers are for. My mother loves me and has been willing to launch tears on my behalf since she first learned that I existed. So what? What do I do with that? Nothing. What can I do with that? Her love was already complete well before I could even begin to respond. And for as long as a mother is a mother, from the first moment to every visit full of discussions about the meaning of life and our fragile grasp on our ideas of what we will do with our days here, there exists a love that has no concern for our utility, because there is so much to revel in regarding what we're worth.

My mother would fight as fiercely for my life and would grieve my death as beautifully and majestically as Danielle has with Aidan, with plenty of passion and plenty of tears. And my knowledge of that fact is not useless knowledge. It reorders the world, and it thrusts me to the top of the value chart — not in a way that competes with other people, but in a way that sure as heck tells me where I stand as compared to my job or the stupid phone bill. Her love calls me to believe that I need no external evidence of utility to make me more valuable, more acceptable. It shows me how silly the idol of my false self is, and how absurd my sense of control. My beautiful idol is worthless in my mother's eyes, as it is worthless in the eyes of my heavenly Father.

God made all of this evident in every mother, and it rings through all eternity every time a child hears his mother say, "Hi, Kiddo."

CHAPTER 30

Why God Invented Dads

I've been working with the retarded guys for over a year now. I earn a thousand dollars per month, and give one hundred dollars to Jon as support for his job at the street school where he teaches Bible and math to kids who have lost their invitation to public schools for one reason or another. The rest? I don't know where it goes, but it's gone as soon as it's mine. Rent, my share of the utilities, food, an occasional movie, a book here and there, and credit card payments. Lots and lots of dollars to the credit card companies, who have stopped raising my limit. I have been picking and choosing which bills to pay for months, and I'm going backward. When I was in Chicago I couldn't find ways to spend all I made, and I know that I haven't reined myself in enough during my time here. Of course, I earned only five thousand dollars the first year I was here and about ten thousand the second, which isn't much.

It's May 26. In a little over two months I'll be twenty-six. I should not be at the end of my financial rope, but I am. I could go and get a real job, but I don't want that. I pick up extra shifts here and there, and I sand and stain the decks of mountain homes with David when it's warm, which helps some, but I don't see a way to keep the job I have and make it financially.

I'm going to have to ask my dad for a loan. I don't know if he'll do it, either. The last time I borrowed money from him, I paid him back so irregularly that it was a lousy experience for both of us. I was in high school then, but the memory still lingers, and I expect he'll feel as though he's learned his lesson. Besides, I could go and get a real job anytime, right? I was the big-shot advertising guy; there must be people lined up to hire a guy like me. He won't actually point those things out, but I feel like that's part of the unspoken dynamic between us. He answers on the third ring.

"Nyellow."

"Hey, Dad."

"Howdy."

"Whatcha doing?" I ask.

"Just about to bring the chicken in from the grill."

"Oh. Well, I don't want to take a lot of your time."

"You're welcome to my time." I hear the screen door to the back deck open and close as he carries the wireless phone with him. "What's up?"

"Well, I've kind of run out of money."

Silence. I hurry forward.

"I'm just making so little that I can't gain ground on old debt. I've got my budget under control, but I'm not even able to pay the minimums on my credit cards anymore."

"Uh-huh." The lid on the grill slams down. I don't hear him pass back through the screen door. He must be standing outside where Mom won't hear the conversation. Not a good sign.

"So what I was hoping is that we could find some sort of loan plan."

"I don't know. Last time wasn't good."

"Dad, that was eight years ago. I'm not the same person anymore."

"You know, part of good stewardship is proactive — you have an obligation to earn enough to get by. I don't think I'd be doing you any favors if I helped you delay learning that," he says.

"I know you think what I'm doing is foolish — "

"I've never said that. This has nothing to do with what you're doing — "

"God pays what God pays, Dad."

"That's not exactly the sort of argument that's going to help you in this conversation."

"I don't want to have to argue for your help. Believe me, I don't like this any more than you do, and I'd go anyplace else for help if it meant I could avoid asking you. But I'm out of options." My voice breaks a little. I hate that. Spoiled brat.

"How much do you need?" he asks.

"Nine thousand. That's the total of my debt. I'd be willing to pay you interest, and I'd be happy to have my paychecks sent to you and to have you send me an allowance so you'd be completely in control of the repayments."

He laughs. "You want to know how interested I am in doing your budget for you and having you come to me every time you want a few extra dollars from your paycheck?"

"So you're saying no."

"I need to think about it. If you need an answer now, it would be no; but let me talk to Mom and I'll get back to you."

"Okay," I say.

"Okay," he says.

"Have a good dinner."

"You too."

I'm trembling with rage and fear and frustration and self-loathing as I hang up the phone.

"Argh!" I yell. At my dad, at God, at myself, at the world I've chosen to trust with this whole path of life, at my own foolish choices, at my vulnerability and weakness. Just flat stupid weakness. I wouldn't want to invest in it either.

But that's what it feels like I'm asking for: an investment. I know that it's his money and that I'm a bad credit risk because I have no idea what I'm building, but isn't there something else worth the money? Isn't there something about what I'm doing that has real value, some value that isn't monetary? I feel like I'm on an important path, and that at some point support for me will have some value, even if the reward doesn't come directly back to the person investing the money. Am I not some sort of conduit to what the kingdom of heaven is doing in the world? I feel like the rules of the worldly economy don't apply to me in the same way. And even if they do, isn't this time in my life worth something, for all I'm learning? I'm scratching at it, but I can't tell if I'm scratching at something real or if I'm just scratching to try to claw my way out of feeling like a failure who's just had to look at how much he's failed and is trying to negotiate a loophole.

The phone rings. That was quick.

"Hello?"

"Hi. My name's Jeff Johnsen. I run Mile High Ministries and was told by Pastor Ellison at Five Points Christian Church that I should meet you."

"Oh? Cool."

"Ellison said he thought you might be a good candidate for a position we're trying to fill downtown. Do you have a minute?"

Uh, ye-ah. "Sure."

"The place is called Bud's Warehouse. Have you heard of it?"

"I don't think so."

"It's sort of like a nonprofit Home Depot. We take in donated building materials and then sell them at very affordable prices, mostly to folks downtown."

"Okay."

"Bud's employees are mostly people coming out of prison or off welfare. We provide a place that teaches them basic skills and then help them find positions elsewhere."

"Sounds cool."

"We think it is. But we've had a hard time getting it rolling. It's been in existence for about two years, and we've had a few real successes with people, but the business itself has struggled. We just lost the executive director, and we're looking for someone who can come in and turn the business around."

"Wow."

"There's a strong board of business people, so there will be plenty of support on that end, but we need someone with passion and energy who can bring in donations and manage employees in a loving way."

"Tell me about the difficulties getting the business rolling," I say.

"Like I said, there's a strong board, and we initially raised $150,000 to get things rolling. But there have been quite a few bumps along the way during the past two years."

"Uh-huh."

"And this is where we're looking for someone who can really come in and grab the reins. This afternoon the checking account balance is at about $13,000."

"Okay."

"And the business is losing roughly $8,000 per month."

"Geez."

"We're committed to making the business work. We wouldn't bring someone new in and only give them a month to make a turnaround."

"So what kind of turnaround time are you committed to?"

"Well, there is no set timeframe. The board is solid, but not everyone agrees that the best option is to continue."

"No pressure there," I quip.

Jeff laughs. "I know it's a lot to consider all at once. But the business model has proven itself in places like Phoenix and Baltimore, so we know it can work."

"Man, to turn an $8,000 a month shortfall around," I say.

"There's more. If Bud's works, we have quite a few other things we'd like to do. The vision is for Bud's to be so successful that it can shoulder the load for other ministry-focused businesses as they get off the ground."

"So the vision isn't just to turn Bud's around."

"Exactly. We're looking for someone who can turn Bud's into a big, fat cash cow."

I laugh at the audacity of the plan.

"I know. It's a long way from where we are today. But the cash cow part brings up another important attribute we're looking for in the new executive director. He or she will have to be willing to work doubly hard, and make Bud's work doubly hard, because there will be more than just the weight of one donation-dependent business to manage. There will be hard choices and times when it seems like the profits that could pull Bud's a step ahead will be diverted into other endeavors over which the executive director will have no control. The person we're looking for will have to be a quick study of people, able to produce on the business front, navigate and manage a board, and be a team player who will submit personal gratification to the needs of the larger effort."

"It sure sounds exciting," I say.

"Would you be interested in getting together for breakfast some-time the first part of next week to talk about it?"

"I'd like that."

"How about the Butcher Block? It's just down the street from Bud's, and I love greasy spoons."

"So do I."

"Say Monday at 8:30?"

"Great. See you then. And thanks for calling."

The interview with Bud's board was intense, and it is definitely split, but I'm willing to take half the salary of the previous executive direc-tor — and they were impressed that I want to live in the room con-nected to the office in the warehouse.

So it looks like I'm pretty much doubling my salary and elimi-nating my rent.

Today is sunny. The birds are singing. For the first time in a long time I'm feeling like I can see a little distance down the path in front of me, and it looks like someplace I want to go. I've spent the day reviewing my budget as best as I can remember it, doing laundry, and even ironing clothes. But one of the details I hadn't really thought about before is that I don't have a car. I'm going to need a car to get to meetings with board members, donors, and with what I'm told is a fairly large and constant number of people in the suburbs who want to learn more about Bud's Warehouse and about urban ministry in general. I can't afford one. I don't see how I'll be able to for a while yet, either. There's no way I'd be approved for a car loan with my outstanding debt and a brand-new job. I haven't heard from my dad, and it looks like I'm going to have to take a pretty big late fee hit before my first Bud's Warehouse check comes in, and that's not going to be good for the credit rating. I've wanted to call home to tell my folks about the job, but want to make sure everything is official first.

I hear the mailman make his delivery outside. In it is a large, fairly thick manila envelope with my parents' address in the corner. Dad has sent Suze Orman books before, about money management and that sort of thing. And I still feel gun-shy from the article Ivy sent. Items that come from Zionsville usually serve mostly to ridicule me and leave me reeling for days. I stare at the envelope without opening it for a moment, assuming from the feel of the contents that my father came across a *Fortune* magazine article whose title he will have circled in the table of contents, and to which he will have attached a yellow sticky note saying something like, "This is the reason you're going to have to learn this lesson on your own." Jerk. He doesn't understand that I don't want to be just like him. He doesn't understand that I've seen something he doesn't see. I think of throwing the envelope into the garbage without even opening it — I don't need that kind of taunting from him right now. Forget it, in a couple of days I'll be able to call home and tell them about the new job. I open the envelope with the intention of finding some line in the article that I can turn back on him later to highlight the shallowness of his world.

Into my hand slide twenty or thirty heavy-gauge pieces of paper, bordered with scrollwork and fancy lettering. There is a note typed on my father's letterhead.

"Enclosed please find stock certificates that today traded for $9,270. This is not a loan. Take this gift and start again. I love you. Dad."

He signed the last word.

PART V

WITH POWER TO FIX THE WORLD

CHAPTER 31

The Cost of Ascending Ministry

"But why?" Henry Love doesn't know why I'd leave. He's twenty-two and has only been living in the program for a year. He's never had a staff person leave.

"Bye bye." Sam Love preempts, angrily. He's six years older than his roommate, and has seen a great many staff people leave. They both feel the upsetting of their worlds deeply. Henry is trying to find a place for it. Sam knows not to bother.

"I'm really going to miss you both," I say. "But we can still go to movies sometimes." I mean it, but I wonder how true this will turn out to be.

"But why you go?" Henry asks again.

"I have another job, Henry Love." I say his name with extra vigor, wanting to connect with the funny game. "I won't be able to work here anymore."

"Don't call, don't call us that," Sam Love — Sam — says. "Don't call him Henry Love, and don't call me Sam Love. That's not our name."

"Stop it!" Henry yells at Sam. "Stop talking like that to him!"

"It's okay, Henry," I say. "It's just a funny name to remind us that we're friends. We'll still be friends, even if Sam doesn't want me to use that name anymore."

"No, we won't," Sam argues. "We won't be friends anymore."

"Stop it, Sam!" Henry slaps Sam.

"No hitting," Sam replies, and then takes a few steps away and begins practicing his air guitar and singing the *Dukes of Hazzard* theme song.

Henry laughs at Sam the Entertainer. They are perfect room-mates. So good for each other.

"Henry, can we still go to movies together after I start working somewhere else?" I ask.

"Yes!" He emphasizes that of course we can and that the question is silly. "I miss you."

"I'll miss you too, Henry," I say, rising from the kitchen table, the Diet Coke I took from their refrigerator in hand. I turn to the front door of their apartment.

"You can leave the soda here," Sam says.

I stop. I've done nothing but consume from the excesses of these gentle men.

"You're right, Sam. I will leave it here." I place the can on the entertainment center. "Better?"

"That's not where it goes," Sam says, still playing the air guitar.

Nailed to the wall by Sam Love. He can't go with me through my convoluted rationalizations, arguments, and far-flung theories and constructs, but he can recognize truth far better than I'll ever be able to.

I carry the Diet Coke to the sink, pour it out, and drop the can in the recycling bag. "Sorry, Sam."

"That's better," he says.

"See ya, Turkey," Henry says, smiling so big I can see his molars.

"See ya, Ham," I say back, and close the door behind me.

I descend the three flights of stairs to the parking lot and am on the sidewalk heading for Vince's apartment when I hear Sam yelling from his balcony.

"See ya, Turkey!"

"Turkey!" Henry echoes.

"Turkey Love!" Sam yells.

I turn and they're both pressed against the rail, waving as though I may not be able to see them. I swear Heaven says farewell in such ways. I wave back like I'm trying to be seen by an airplane. Someone of normal IQ is parking her car beside me, and I couldn't care less.

"See ya, Turkey Lips!" I scream back at them.

For a moment I am every father who ever left a crying child in a window as he headed off to work for the day and was greeted eagerly upon his return in the evening. I have stolen a trusting heart, caused it pain for the connection, and have been forgiven. I have done so much wrong. I have said I was doing the best I could when in truth I was only doing the best I was willing to do. I know better. I could defend myself against other people, but I cannot defend myself against my own doubts. But I am willing to accept the waving and laughter of two retarded men as the summary word on the matter, at least for now.

Vince, on the other hand. Vince, and his heart. The heart he listens to. The heart that tells him he is loved. The heart that risked with me. The heart that knew the companionship and the joy of feeling normal with me. The heart that trusted me far more than a man of greater mental acuity would have. Vince. I broke his heart. He did not get angry. He did not plead. He did not ask questions. He did not cry. He just looked at me as though he was waiting for the punch line. He listened and nodded and went quietly to his room and lay down on his bed.

When I took this job, I felt like I was being led through some learning experiences. And I have seen some ugly things about myself that I may not have seen otherwise. But this cannot continue. There is something profoundly wrong about the way I see the world and about the way I make my choices. Or about the way I made the choices that got me to this place, where I have to break hearts to move on. I don't care what sort of "that's just the way it is" rationalizations rule the world; it's not right to inflict wounds for the sake of progress.

Am I worth the pain I cause? Is the good I want to do at the new job worth the pain I'm leaving with Vince? What sort of damage will I do to the next set of people? How am I supposed to be doing this whole thing?

CHAPTER 32

Benevolent White Moses

On a wintry Wednesday evening about a year and a half ago, I had to leave the church service because the tears were coming on and I didn't want to make a scene. I ended up in the parking lot, absolutely bawling. I wanted to be used. I was past the whole deal about wanting God to take my life or have me die and go to heaven, but I very much wanted to be used in some unique and meaningful manner. I was also convinced that the manner of my utilization should be somehow in line with the skills and abilities God had given me.

But I felt like my life was being rejected, or at the very least that it was taking too long. I ended up standing in the snow, and angrily saying, "Well, I'm not letting go. I don't care how long you shake me and ignore me, I'm not letting go." In my mind I had pictures of those little dogs people drag around the kitchen floor on home video shows. I was going to be one of those. I could control my determination to lock my jaws. Still I sobbed within my grief and self-righteous desires for what felt like twenty minutes or so, until I was finally distracted by the huge amounts of snot with which my nose was blowing bubbles. Even my most sublime moments end in interruption by the mundane, and the mundane is almost never flattering.

Bud's Warehouse, burning and rapidly sinking ship that it is, with rats swimming away from the flaming wreckage and looking in scornful disbelief over their shoulders at me as I swim toward it, may well turn out to be the place where my prayers will be answered.

Of course I have just about zero credibility with my new employees. We aren't exactly part of the same demographic. There are currently three employees: Juan, Marcos, and Hector. All of them grew up in rough worlds. Juan, now in his early twenties, was an Olympic hopeful in boxing who lost his opportunity when he fell into a street fight and got sideways with the law. Marcos is in his late forties, with a salt-and-pepper ponytail, a patch over one eye, and scars from where acid was spilled on him in a fight when he was in prison. He usually wears a black leather motorcycle vest and boots. He also has a black T-shirt with an American flag on it, beneath which is written "Try burning this one, sucker." He can't read, but he's the only one who speaks Spanish, which helps in roughly half of our sales. Hector is about three months out of prison and is definitely the meanest and toughest of the three, though I have no idea who would win in a fight among them.

The warehouse is in an area controlled by an LA street gang called the Crips. Their color is blue. Their rival gang, the Bloods, wears the color red. A couple of days ago, Hector was standing on the sidewalk outside the warehouse waiting for his ride home. In a red sweatshirt. A car full of Crips passed on the one-way street, whipped fiercely around, and came to a screeching halt on the sidewalk about two feet from Hector. A young black man leapt from the passenger side and leveled a shotgun at Hector.

"Don't you know where you are, boy?" the kid with the gun demanded.

Hector didn't even move the sole of his shoe from the wall against which he was leaning. He didn't even take the cigarette from his mouth. He started his response with the sound of air brakes. "Tss. Get lost, Stupid. I don't play little gangbanger games."

The young man with the shotgun yelled threats at Hector and climbed back into the car, which pealed out backward, spun around, and screamed away in the direction it had originally been heading.

Juan, Marcos, and I had been standing about fifty feet away, in the open garage door on the same street. They had both been ready to fight. I'd pulled my cell phone from my pocket and flipped it open to be ready to call 911 from a good hiding place. After the car sped away, they went and shook wrists with Hector, exclaiming what a tough guy he was. I went to my office and signed us up for an alarm system with silent alarm buttons that can be worn looped over a person's belt.

But that's cool, our differences. I may end up learning from them how to deal with immediate threats, and they may end up learning from me how to live in a way that brings a person into fewer conflicts. We'll all learn something about life and God and the things we have in common and how they're more powerful and more important than the things that make us different.

If there is one thing that I've always felt, it's the sense of being different. Usually not better, just different. Life in Denver has given me the same feeling, but even more potently so. When a person does ministry, it is exactly his differences that enables him to do the ministry, though it is people's universal similarities in respect to struggle that bind us together enough to bother with one another. The trick is what to make of those differences, and what an honest assessment of those differences means in terms of obligation to action.

I've been thinking a lot about Moses, an Israelite who grew up living as a sort of royal stepchild to the pharaoh. But he identifies with his people, who are slaves in Egypt. As an educated, affluent member of the ruling class in America, I've grown up living much like an Egyptian in that it is my people who hold the higher position in this culture. It is a race thing to a great extent, but mostly it's a class thing, and I'm from the upper class. I'm also the eldest of three sons, and there were a great many times I was left to watch over my brothers. During those times, or to lesser degrees at school every day, their well-being was in my hands. Pick on me, and who knows how things will go. Pick on my brothers, and I'm coming after you.

It's easy with brothers, but it's harder to know what a person's duty is to people your parents don't teach you to see as your responsibility. Moses knew he had a connection to the Jewish slaves, but I don't imagine there were a whole lot of father-and-son discussions in the royal den about compassion and empowerment of the poor. At least I assume there weren't; there were none in my house growing up. It's not surprising to me that it took Moses until he was an adult to make his stand; there is a great potential cost in identifying with the people upon whose backs one's own world has been built.

But there came a day when Moses saw an Egyptian beating a Jewish slave, and on that day Moses knew the Jew was his brother. And his brother was being beaten by someone who, for whatever reason, was not Moses's brother. That's the day everything changed, and Moses had no idea it was about to happen.

Today, especially in the cultures of boundaries and bootstraps and therapeutic preoccupations that run rampant in ministry circles, people talk about a cute and quaint love for the underdog, but this is not a real love. If I was Moses and my brother was being beaten in front of me, in today's Christian world I would be expected — under threat of malicious whispers delivered behind my back in the form of prayer request — to go and shield the slave, to embrace him without removing him from the situation, and to take the blows on my back if I was really feeling like a hero martyr. From that posture of shared submission, of identification with the beating, I would be expected to ask what my brother had done to receive these blows. I would recognize the authority of the man with the club, and I would submit to his authority as I sought to dissuade him from his course of action. He's the one with the club, after all, and I've been taught that the man with the club, in whatever form the club may appear and deliver its abuse, is usually in the right.

Not Moses. Moses sees an Egyptian beating his brother, and he kills the dude, dead, and stuffs him in the sand.

Many of the people I serve at Bud's Warehouse have made mistakes, and there is a right and just debt to be paid for the mistakes we make. The trick is this, though: Abuse is never justice. And the people who live with, or are raised by, people who are not in the ruling class are at a twofold disadvantage. The first is that they don't make the rules about what is a mistake. I don't mean moral things; I mean the consequences of trusting people and systems who lie and laugh behind their *buyer beware* slogans, who withhold credit, concern, and compassion for people whose worlds teach an entirely different sort of common sense. The system, which exists in spite of what an incendiary phrase "the system" has become, has been and will always be built and maintained by people with something to preserve and something to gain, to the exclusion and loss of people who are unable to fight back in the same ways. The rules, and the understandings that work to measure mistake from wisdom, are the property and purview of the people who create the rules and have the power to enforce them.

The second disadvantage experienced by the people I'm here to serve is exactly what the Jewish slave experienced, which is an inability to achieve justice without the aid of a guide or a liberator. This dynamic makes the wait for justice interminably long, and the waiting is a warping experience that leads to despair far more often than it leads to deliverance. What's more, there is a tremendous cost in admitting that someone else must help if the person being beaten is ever going to be liberated. When a person admits such a thing, they immediately fall to the mercy of their deliverer. Most of the time the person or organization that shows up offering deliverance services one day is the same person or organization that will press charges or steal your money the next. If a person is not in the ruling class, if they don't know the rules of the game, it's nearly impossible for them to be anything but casualties of the game. That's abuse, not justice.

My job, and the task of Bud's Warehouse, is to bring knowledge of the system and the resources of the ruling class to bear for the sake of people who otherwise will know little but abuse in their lives. My job is not to be a living shield for the men in my employ, or for the people who comprise my neighborhood and customer base. My job is not to find out what they've done and negotiate for fewer blows from the Egyptian overlord. My job is to knock the dude out, and it's entirely possible that the differences between my brothers and me will forever be so great that they don't see what has been done for them. That's fine, because in the end this isn't even about them, any more than the response of Moses was about the experience of the individual Jewish slave being abused. The response is about doing what is right with the position and ability granted to Moses, or to me, or to the Bud's board, by Providence.

This, as I said before, feels like it could be an incredible answer to my prayer to be used, and I've moved past the point in my experience where being the white stranger shamed me into shaving my head. Now I wear my hair in a crisp left-handed part, and in the past four months we've made this business go forward to the tune of donation receipts closing in on six figures. I'm a yuppie tooling around Denver in a white Saturn sedan, clubbing Egyptians, and buying justice for men who've never known it before.

CHAPTER 33

Murmurs of Revolution

The new job is going well, and Bud's is seeing some real success, but there's something disquieting about it all. I think it goes deeper than what some friends call my tendency to sabotage my own successes. I hear cracking lately — in my soul — and I'm terrified that my scaffolding is about to collapse and send me even further into my dark well. I think the cracking started about two weeks ago.

I'm still flat broke, and that morning I'd received a card from my grandmother back in Zionsville. In it were the words, "I'm proud of you" and a one-hundred-dollar bill. An hour later a Latina woman in her midtwenties, with long hair and a few extra pounds from childbearing, made her way into the warehouse from the driving snow. She was wearing black tights, cheap open-toed shoes with clear plastic straps criss-crossing the top of her foot, and a light jacket. In the stroller was a baby, a girl of maybe six months. Trailing on her coattails were two boys, probably three and five years old. Their noses were red and running, and they hid behind their mother. The

woman was trying not to cry, but it was clear that the cold and something else were driving her to the edge. She told me that they'd been
living with her father, but he'd kicked them out of his house that
morning. She'd just earned ten dollars for cleaning the office of a
man down the street, and asked if I would be willing to pay her to do
the same. I looked at the kids, and at her feet. I wanted to help her,
but I was not about to pay her ten dollars to clean my office while
her kids sat and watched, and then send them all back out into the
snow. I refused, but pulled my grandmother's money from my pocket
and handed it to her, telling her to go and get a hotel room, to get
herself and her kids out of the snow, to get warm and take the day to
figure out what she would do next. She cried profusely. I told her to
pay me back when she could, that she knew where to find me, and
that I'd be around. Then she took her kids and headed back out into
the snow.

Every night since then I've dreamed of that woman. Usually,
I'm running after them through the snow, slipping on the ice, unable to catch them. I want to do more. She told me her name was
Maria, but I want to know her last name. I want to know where her
father lives. I want to know which hotel they're going to use. I want
to know that the kids will be warm. I want her not to cry. I want her
to know she's not alone. I want to help her get out of whatever cycle
has brought her to such a state. I race after them, feeling as though
I've failed and am desperate to make things right.

Each night the dreams have become more desperate, and more
about me. More about my helplessness and my ugliness. I've felt my
panic, driven by my inability to provide any real help to her or her
kids, and something about that inability profoundly threatens my
sense of self and worth.

And then last night.

Last night I dreamed that I was raping her in a dead-end alley. Her kids watched and the brick walls ran in blood under dark, dreaming clouds. We were already in the act, and the only violence was the recognition of the situation in which we were engaged. There was a look in her eyes—the same eyes that had wept in gratitude only days ago—and with every motion, the look showed that something she already knew was being confirmed by my choices. By my actions. By my presence, even. My existence. It enraged and terrified me, but something about my actions was scripted and I could not stop. Each moment that passed was some twisted moment of ferocious victory for her, as though she knew it would go this way all along. I did not understand what she was proving, or why she hated me. I had helped her—I'd been her friend. Why would she feel such monstrous things about me? She did not fight, and I was horrified that this was all happening in front of her kids, and she didn't seem to be bothered. On the contrary, the cries of her children seemed to prove to her that she was successfully teaching her children a hard lesson about people like me. The terror and the rage of the nightmare were too awful for me, and I made myself wake up.

What is that thing some people, usually women, know? That victory in violation? Is it a fear confirmed, horror chosen as satisfaction over the even more terrifying voice of faith that calls us away from fear? Is the arrival of the nightmare better than its threat? How do I know it enough to build a dream around it? Is it true of men, of power, of women, of vulnerability, of fear, of humanity, of God? What is it? Why are there so many people living like Maria in the world? How is it that so many truths can be expressed in their choosing of their own fierce destruction?

Is it what I was after back when I wanted to get shot? Is it what I seek with women? With ministry? Worse yet, is it something I inspire in other people — people I want to serve but end up hurting?

How far does this nightmare reach, and why is there this rage within people like me who feel a hellish ambivalence about serving, saving, or raping weakness in its pathetic apathy. After Moses fights to save one Jew, the others ask just who he thinks he is.

Just like Hungarian Vince's father must still be asking about me, the guy who let his son down.

Or Rachel.

Or my old gay roommate.

Or my family.

It's a good question.

Just who do I think I am?

CHAPTER 34

Uh, About That Moses Thing . . .

I'm not Moses. And I think maybe Bud's is the perfect answer to a hero's prayer I don't pray anymore. I live in a filthy room adjacent to the filthy office in a filthy warehouse in a filthy part of town. I love well, and I give richly from a reserve that fills from the throne of heaven, and my work is changing the lives of the men who work here, but it's not because I'm great. I'm playing a role, and all too often that results-focused role leaves me feeling about as filthy as the place where I live and work.

First a word about the place.

The carpets make people motion sick until they realize the motion is actually a complex pattern of industrious migratory ants. The cockroaches are kept in check by the black widow spiders in the corners. That smell is the sewers of this industrial neighborhood backing up into my shower. The snoring sound is one of the men who sleeps right outside my grate-clad window on the covered loading dock. I spend my nights fearing those men and any other noise I hear in the giant, gray building.

Rare would be the evening when I would not be found, along with my little white car, locked within the warehouse. This is the result of having no good, quick, or safe way to enter through the large garage doors without leaving myself, my car, or the warehouse unduly vulnerable to the malevolence of the area's interlopers. Faith and fear race up opposing sides of the same mountain, and whichever one gets to the top first wins the ability to stop the other in its tracks.

Dress and act like a White Moses; run scared like a White Moses.

Ah, but the daytime. I live for the daytime, when the smog-shrouded moon's Kryptonic trance lifts, the doors of my lair roll open wide, and my powers return. I am the king of breakfast meetings, and lunch meetings, and even multiples of each. And what makes me the king is my ability to spin every moment and each fear, each sacrifice and every hopeful success, into fundraising, vision-casting anecdotes. Wool to gold. Men in ties shake their heads about my lifestyle, and donations are never, ever more than a day or two away. That's if the men in ties escape the meal without writing a check on the spot.

"Do you know what a mule driver is?" I ask the chubby suburbanite who recently sold a flourishing business and is now looking for clues about moving from "success to significance."

"Only if you're talking about the hike down into the Grand Canyon." The chubby suburbanite strains the words through a too-large bite of his first two-dollar breakfast burrito, which he will not order with coffee next time.

"When a drug dealer is transporting drugs from one place to another, it's common practice to hire someone else to drive the vehicle. For longer distances, there will be multiple drivers, each driving a leg."

"So the drivers meet someplace and hand over the car to the next guy?"

"Yeah."

"How does the first driver get home?" Chubby is all about systems.

"I don't know. It doesn't matter," I reply. "What does matter is that Marcos is a mule driver on the weekends a couple of times a month."

"Marcos is the one with the ponytail and the eye patch, right?"

"Right."

"Wow."

"Yeah. So here's the dilemma. Obviously that sort of work isn't what we're looking to have our employees do."

"Right."

"But we know that it's exactly what they'd do — or at least he'd do — if he was no longer a Bud's employee."

"Okay."

"So, what's the solution? How should Bud's respond now that he's told me about it with the assumption that I won't use it against him?"

"Did you tell him you'd keep it a secret?" the chubby businessman asks, wincing at the taste of his coffee after a mouthful of salsa.

"No, but that's not really the point."

"I guess not. So you have to find some way to make him choose against it."

"Right."

"And you can't coerce the choice."

"Right. I can't give him an ultimatum, or I'll lose the invitation to engage with his world."

"It's sort of like having a teenager," the businessman says.

"Maybe. More like having a teenager who's already run away and is willing to meet you for lunch and a little advice and allowance once a week, but who refuses to be owned by the allowance. And he's not a teenager; he's a man with gray hair who has made plenty of adult choices and has experienced more things in his life than I have, and is far more street savvy than most people."

"That would be different."

"But you know things won't end well for Marcos if he keeps taking these risks. He's at the bottom of the food chain. He doesn't even have a driver's license, and he can't read, and he's poor enough that he doesn't have a whole lot of walk-away money saved up. Plus, he's already very much a part of a culture that works that way."

"Wow."

"Yeah, wow. That's why what we're doing is so important in the lives of the men who work at Bud's. It goes far beyond teaching them to show up to work or how to drive a forklift or run a cash register. What we're really doing is introducing these men to a whole different way of interacting with the world, and showing them a whole part of society that works from an entirely different paradigm than they do."

The chubby businessman who has been looking for something significant to do with his time and money, looking for a return on his success, is thinking now. "Yeah."

"In his world the biggest studs are the people at the top of the food chain, which means people who have made great money as their own bosses, answering to nobody."

The chubby businessman laughs. "Entrepreneurs answer to more people than anybody else does."

"That may be, but that's sure not how Marcos or the other guys see it. They assume that you've taken big chances, have made smart choices, and have kicked butt along the way. Their world works more like a wolf pack, where the dominant wolf is the one to follow. They'd see you as a dominant wolf. Power sells. Power earns you the right to speak into their worlds. And you can do it in ways that I cannot. I'm their boss, not their hero or their role model. The best I can do is to make them feel like they're part of something that's succeeding and then introduce them to people who represent a world they'd choose over the one they already know."

"Is that all?" he asks facetiously. "That's a lot. That's a big deal."

I know that reflected affirmation is the green light for the big ask. The chubby businessman is sold on turning his success into significance at Bud's Warehouse, where his success is applauded and his opportunity to make a difference is clearly marked. It's a big, shiny gem to affix to his shell, and he's being sold by a resurgent, increasingly prostitutional advertising professional who's been known to lie just to see if he can get away with it. The chubby businessman is an easy mark — even easier than teenagers looking for permission and protection to explore irresponsible sex. He's already covered his shell in the other stuff — this whole altruistic-dominant-wolf things gleam from a mile away.

He doesn't know it yet, but his bank account has already dropped ten thousand dollars, and more will come during the next year.

"It is a big deal," I say. "It's a life-changing deal not only for the individuals who encounter a better option here, but also for their families and their communities who will see the aggressive risk takers like Marcos turn their lives around instead of getting caught and thrown in prison. My job is to be the bridge between driven men who have achieved something in their lives, and driven men with something to prove. Men who only need a mentor to absolutely revolutionize their worlds."

The chubby businessman is nodding. I watch the squint of his eyes to gauge how much to ask. The chubby man doesn't look away.

He squints a little tighter. No need to go for the cash in this meeting — a little tour will bring him into the fold. And it really is about recruitment, not money. The primary benefit of getting the donation is that it keeps the connection active and the prospects of additional collaboration strong. Though the secondary benefit is that if one person gives and I return to the board with the good news, other people are more likely to buy in further. Nothing generates success like success. Nothing sells jewelry or shell decoration like jewelry or shell decoration on someone else.

"You say you want to reorient your world from success to significance. I can help you do that, and I can help you make sense of it in ways that right now are only vague hunches. And where I can't help you, I have a team of maybe two dozen men who have either been where you are, or are themselves right where you are, and they will make this whole reorientation real and concrete for you so it doesn't slip from you as the distractions of your ordinary life come and weaken your grip on this moment of clarity in your career."

The businessman knows he's being closed, but the power is still his, and he's ready for the bottom line. I finish my Mountain Dew and look for the waitress. I always do this to break the tension. It allows me to come back to the situational table I've set, but to return to it sitting on the same side as the person — let's just call him the mark — with whom I am seeking to establish an action-based relationship.

"Donna," I call, and lift my cup at the waitress, who smiles and agrees to bring me a refill. I turn back to the businessman. "Did I tell you she's a descendant of Martin Luther's?"

"No."

"Yeah. I was reading *The Bondage of the Will* in here one morning and she told me. But she had no idea who Luther was. All she knew was that her grandmother had told her they were related.

She was pretty impressed to learn what an important man he was. Ever since then when I walk in here she arrives at the table with a Mountain Dew before I even sit down."

The businessman watches Donna filling a scratched red cup with the yellow soda at the fountain. I continue.

"What I'm hoping to find for Marcos is someone who can impress him, spend some time with him, and introduce him to a world that makes better sense than being a mule driver."

The businessman nods.

"I picture you riding along with him as he picks up donations one day. Just spend the time together and see what happens. I'd encourage you to listen to the details of his life outside of Bud's and see where you can offer practical advice or help, and then make your way in as the alpha wolf would protect a subordinate. Don't think of it as a paternalistic thing — he's not a kid — but do stay clear in your mind that what he'll respond to is power, especially power wisely applied. If you find something, let your action be flashier than you'd let it be in Littleton. Flash is power in his world."

"I can do that," the businessman says, in a tone similar to the way he would say, "I could afford that" if I'd asked him about a hypothetical ability to purchase a building or an expensive vehicle. I know there's no reason to make the businessman feel like a novice in the land of significance when there exists the option to work from the businessman's comfort in the land of success.

"But make sure you dress in clothes you'd be willing to throw away when the day is done," I say, laughing. "The Bud's van is missing a back window from where the homeless guys broke in so they could sleep in it, and it's also doubled as a toilet more than once."

"Really?" the businessman asks.

"Oh, yeah. You'll love it. It'll probably bring back memories from when you were getting your business off the ground. There are holes rusted through the floor, and the brakes barely work. I tell you, the whole engine only keeps running because Marcos won't let it die. A couple of weeks ago he climbed into the driver's seat and got stuck by a needle someone had left behind."

"Did he get tested for HIV?" the businessman asks, alarmed.

"Yeah, it came back negative. But I don't know if it would show up right away anyway. Do you?"

"No."

Two days later I introduced Marcos to the chubby businessman who recently sold his company. They spent the day driving around the metro area picking up donated building materials. The following Tuesday a nearly new box truck was delivered to the loading dock, driven by a smiling, rather chubby man who has since helped Marcos secure his driver's license, insurance, and weekend work that doesn't involve mule driving. And I've gained yet another anecdote to sell the vision of Bud's Warehouse. Ministry, it would seem, is all about selling. I'm tortured by the fact that I don't know how to do this whole good deal — this worthy cause — purely. Is this a burden every leader has to learn to pay? Is this a weight that is built into the system of things — the whole "heavy is the head that wears the crown" thing? The conflict seems part and parcel with getting results.

"Don't hate the player; hate the game" — as the other pimps say.

CHAPTER 35

WHAT CHRISTIANS IN THE MEXICAN MAFIA ALREADY KNOW

"I know exactly how you feel," my boss, Jeff, says. "And I don't have any good answers to share."

"So you see how creepy this stuff can be?" I ask.

"Yeah. I think anyone who does ministry for very long hits the same wall."

"I feel like I'm manipulating donors and betraying the people I'm supposed to be helping."

"It's lousy to feel like you're pursuing something pure, right, and perfect only to realize that even in the best kitchen some eggs get broken."

"I don't see any way around it — and broken eggs hardly guarantee an omelet will be born," I say. Suddenly, I remember what Ellison told me about Pastor Arrington. "I can only be as honest as the moment is."

"I'll tell you a story. It won't make the confusion go away, but it may help you see it better."

I push my napkin under the plate with my smothered burrito on it, showing Jeff I'm ready to listen.

"I met a man a few years ago who is a big deal in the Mexican mafia. I was with a small group of urban ministry leaders in Mexico City, and our host told us he wanted us to meet this guy. There were maybe seven of us who went together to this man's office — more like a small palace — above a downtown nightclub. There were armed guards everywhere, and it was about the most intimidating place I've ever been."

"I bet."

"Well, it turns out this man had become a Christian a year before we visited him. He'd grown up in a Catholic culture, but he never knew Jesus. He had an amazing conversion story, but that's not important here. What is important was that this guy suddenly had this dilemma. What to do with his job? It's not like the Mexican mafia plays nice, or does a whole lot of philanthropic work. Of course, we were all biting our tongues because there was no way we could see how he could possibly stay in his job."

"So how did he justify it?" I ask.

"He couldn't, of course. But he was really over a barrel. First off, he thought that he would be allowed to live if he tried to get out, but he wasn't sure. That wasn't the hard part for him, though. The hard part was that he knew if he quit, someone else would step right into his position. And that person wouldn't have the same internal conflicts about what he was doing. Getting out not only wouldn't solve the problem, it would probably make it worse."

"But that wouldn't be his responsibility."

"Wouldn't it?" Jeff asks.

"So what did the guy do?"

"I don't know what happened later, but at the time the best he'd been able to conclude was that he was going to stay in his place to influence as much change as he could — to create a 'kinder, gentler Mexican mafia' — and then when he could do no more, he would get out."

"That's a lot to swallow," I say.

"I thought so, too, at the time. But on the flight home what struck me is that in many ways I'm doing exactly the same thing. I think that's what our host wanted us to have to struggle with."

"But it's not like you're having people killed."

"No," Jeff says. "But the Mexican mafia makes no claim to being a gatekeeper between this life and communion with God in the next."

"Neither do we," I say.

"Not explicitly, but you know as well as I do that some of the people who come around looking to help or donate are really looking to buy indulgences. They want you to tell them some stories, to tell them how much good their gift is going to do. They're looking for ways to be right with God, and to the extent that we let them see us as a way to do that, we play the role of intermediary between them and God. We may be friendly, and the gates may not be locked, but we're gatekeepers just the same."

"So what's the solution?" I ask.

"I don't think there is one," Jeff says. "If I quit on Mile High, or if you quit on Bud's, someone else will step into the same place, and that person may not struggle with managing the power they have over people in a loving manner. If I shut Mile High down or if you decide we should pull the plug on Bud's, another ministry will be planted in the same place with the same dilemma. I think the best we can do is what the Mexican mafia boss is doing — take it where we can take it, live in the fire of the dilemma, and mitigate the damage as best we can, admitting that the system is flawed."

"You have so many years invested in Mile High now. If you'd known all of this when you were first starting, would you have still started it?"

"All I cared about doing was serving inner-city people as though they were Jesus. I just wanted to love them and care for them. Is the system perfect? No. Has the organization benefited people? Yes. But it doesn't do any good to ask if I'd do it all again. I don't know. What I do know is that a lot of good has come from being here. I pray that more good has come than bad, but it's a prayer because I'm not always sure which there's been more of. But no matter what, the good hasn't come for free."

"How's that for truth?" I mutter.

"Not soft, is it?" he asks.

"Not soft," I say.

CHAPTER 36

When Questions Outgrow Solutions

"What are we supposed to do with our lives, then?" Skinny Robert asks as we wander through the rough at Haystack golf course looking for another lost ball.

"I don't know. Maybe it's enough to live as though life were for real, not just something to do while we wait for heaven. What kind of ball were you playing?"

"Titleist three."

"I mean, imagine if being a Christian were about life, and not about mastering the formula for Christian living. And why, by the way, is there a difference between living and Christian living? And why is Christian living so much smaller?"

"So how would your life be different if you bought this?" he asks.

"You should just take the stroke penalty and drop a new ball."

"Not with lunch for you riding on the game. Answer the question."

"I wouldn't do professional ministry, for starters."

"Wow. Really? Why?"

"It's too compartmentalized for me. It's not right to hire special-ists to care for people, or to sell other believers on helping. It's not personal, or real."

"So you'd say forget the people you're helping? Right there — is that it?"

"That's a leaf. I don't think I'd even know the people I help. It's weird that we even know each other now. But if I got involved with a place like Bud's, I wouldn't interact with them as a representative of an organization. I'd do it just as a part of my regular life, as part of what I'd choose to be as a follower of Jesus in the lives of people whose paths I crossed. I think that would be vastly more honest."

"Honest?"

"Yeah. Right now the fact is that I need the Bud's employees more than they need me — and Bud's needs them more than they need Bud's."

"How?"

"Drop a ball already."

"Fine. But how do you need the employees more than they need Bud's?"

"Bud's needs to make money to pay my salary, and it needs to make money to stay in business. Staying in business meets an emotional need for the board — it makes them feel like they're doing something productive with their faith, something they can point to when they tally up what sort of person they are. We may be doing some good things for some people, but our real focus is ourselves, not God and not the people we're helping. If Bud's didn't exist, and neither did other ministries or places where a person could contrib-ute and get their 'good Christian' points, what do you think would happen?"

"I think the whole world would burn," Robert says as he swings. "I bet I lost that one too. That's four balls in three holes."

"You're not what they call 'good at the golf.' I bet most people think the end of ministry would be a bad thing too. But I don't think so — not if the Holy Spirit is real. I think the Spirit would continue to convict people and individuals would do things on their own. I think that's how a lot of ministries get started in the first place — one person feels a burden from God to address a situation, usually a specific situation, and pretty soon other people are drawn to it and it takes on a life of its own."

"And it becomes a hiding place," Robert says.

"Yeah, it's all about protecting the beautiful idol. At least that's what I'm thinking right now," I say. "It seems like the raw material in the ministry economy is need. The consumer of this raw material, which is refined into the form of vision-driven programs, is the affluent person who is willing to buy however many 'good Christian' points they feel it will take to cover them with God. I'm the merchant and salesperson. In the end Marcos and the other guys are strip mines I pick at for the raw materials I can trade for donations and donor comfort, and we don't think much about how we are really tearing down the world by making everyone weaker."

"How are you doing that?"

"I make donors weaker by giving them cheap solutions to deep, God-based needs. I sell them hiding places. If the appetite to impact the world originates with God, then it must be a healthy desire. But I get in the way when I come along like a McDonald's or a Wal-Mart, selling junk that's either unhealthy or else of a quality that will never do the job for long. I sell them an easy out, junk food, products with a one-week warranty that are cheaper to replace than repair. I make addictions worse." I grunt on the last word as I tee off.

"Nice shot. What about the Bud's guys? How are you making them weaker?"

"By undermining their worlds. Take Juan, for example. The other day we got onto the subject of welfare. He grew up in the projects and the bulk of his family's income came from welfare. His dad is a great guy — a hardworking carpenter — but for various reasons they've usually worked it so they were on welfare and Juan's dad got paid in cash."

"Okay."

"Well, as we were talking, it became clear that I, and the people I represent, see welfare not only as a line between success and failure, but also as a reflection of flawed character, the difference between a valuable member of society and a drain upon society. At best it's a safety net a person may need to fall into in times of great distress, much like we'd look at bankruptcy or rehab or something like that. Those things leave an indelible mark that forever remains a legitimate basis for evaluating a person. Sort of like how felons are let out of prison but aren't allowed to vote anymore. But Juan's perspective was that it was free money and only a fool would reject the chance to get it."

"Seriously?"

"Yeah. But if I get him to agree that it's a character issue, he has to come to some pretty harsh conclusions about his father and about nearly everyone he's ever known. Is it a noble goal to convince Juan to choose the congratulations offered by me or the board over his loyalty and wholehearted acceptance of his family? It's laughable to think that he would ever do that. In his world, unlike mine and the one in which I was raised, people rate higher than principles. What he gets, that we don't, is that principles are not always the same thing as truth. And truth, from the Trinity on down, does not exist outside of relationship."

"Whoa."

"And for whatever practical realities may be worth considering about welfare and generational change and all of that, we don't have enough of a relational context to truly be part of a cultural shift. We're buying and selling commodities of our own choosing and design, and ultimately we're not interested in what they want — we're only interested in what we want to sell them."

"Harsh."

"Only because we don't see it. We're completely blind to the fact that the people for whom we do ministry are little more than blank slates upon which we seek to write our own legacies. It's the way power has always hidden itself in the guise of love. What's worse is that we're trying to sell our own twisted take on God to these guys too. And it's dangerous ground when rich men show up to introduce poor men to Jesus, whatever the books they sell to rich people may say about being poor in spirit, not in gold."

"Right."

"But I have the power, and I'm the conduit to a very hungry consumer base, and part of what sells is the exportation of educated, affluent white Christianity. Ask anyone around the world. Ask the Starbucks manager in Tehran."

"If it's so bad, they could quit any time. I think you're taking on stuff you can't blame yourself for. It seems like life happens in a context, and the context is flawed, not you."

"Kind of. I'm the one writing the paychecks. I've been granted the power. That means I can do whatever is legal and will be tolerated by my employees. The ways in which I speak into the lives of the men at Bud's Warehouse are my prerogative, and if dealing with that while doing a day's work is not worth the six-and-a-quarter an hour we offer, the men can go find another job and I'll talk about how we grew them until they outgrew the place and call it a success. There will always be more employees willing to take my branding iron for a time. Men will line up to have the board, the business, the donors who learn their secrets without their permission, and the rest of us write our names upon them as though they have become our artwork, our possession signed and displayed to our glory. If you ask me, that sounds an awful lot like dependence. In so many ways it's much worse than a simple job where wages are unreasonably low. We're buying our way into lives to shape them into the image of our own dysfunction. We're doing it in God's name, and we have polished it nicely, but in the end what we're really doing is going out of our way to put something between ourselves and God."

"I still don't see the alternative, though."

"That's only evidence of how wrong the whole model has become. In a fallen world where everything else gravitates to the weakest, lowest common denominator, why would we ever think this area, which is so consistent across so many different sorts of ministries, is one place where not only have we gotten it right, but nearly everyone else has too?"

PART VI

ADMISSIONS UNTO CONVERSION

CHAPTER 37

DEATH OF THE HERO

Here's the rule for how stories are supposed to go: The hero begins in his ordinary world, like Frodo living in the Shire or Luke Skywalker fixing droids in the desert. A crisis is introduced, often by a gatekeeper character who explains that the hero must leave the ordinary world to slay a dragon or find a magic elixir or do some other remarkable thing to save the people of the ordinary world. The hero wishes there could be some other way, but strikes out into the adventure because there is no other way. Everything rides on the ordinary character successfully performing in the new role of hero.

And Luke Skywalker isn't the only one who performs the role of hero. We, the audience, also try out the hero's role. We watch the hero through the lens of our own experiences, and we evaluate how the hero performs. We see ourselves in that position, and we think about what we'd do. We practice being heroes for a while.

Once we get a feel for the lay of the land and for the way the hero tends to respond to the trials he inevitably faces, and once we know which resources the hero can muster for the fighting of trolls or stormtroopers or what-have-you, we're ready to set our sights on the Big Showdown.

Jesus walks around turning water into wine and healing people and preaching about doing unto others, and we get a sense of what he's like. We see him deliver the smackdown on Peter or the Pharisees here and there.

I get to see myself leave the ordinary world of Chicago and capitalist assumptions. I get to test my clever thoughts about collector crabs and sponge crabs, about me and women and my family and God and how much I pray and what a good boy I can be. I get to learn something about the weapons or resources I can apply in my journey and my battle. I get to see what nice and poetic things I can write and come to understand when my real-life best friend's baby dies, or when a homeless mother of three needs immediate help staying out of the real-life snow, or when I interact with employees or board members or God or demons in the all-too-real night. It's all part of the hoops, all part of preparing for the Big Showdown.

Then the good part comes. We get to see the hero suit up, dig down, kick butt, and push through. We get to see what happens when an ordinary person from the ordinary world leaves the ordinary world to become a hero and then engages an enemy who draws the hero beyond himself. Luke turns off the heads-up display and uses the Force. Frodo is swept to rescue by giant eagles. Jesus didn't "rise" from the dead — he was "raised." Oh, yeah — that's the good stuff. Things will be okay, and the hero will come through. We watch that and we feel better about the chances that we'll come through. God will send his eagles. The Spirit will make fighting Satan feel just like shooting womprats back home in Beggar's Canyon. We want to know it will be okay, and that we will be rewarded by the magic beyond ourselves if we will only keep plugging away until the moment when we reach the end of ourselves and our abilities to fight.

"To thine own self be true."

"God helps those who help themselves."

The list of clichés goes on — our entire worldview is built upon the pattern of the hero's journey. Even our Christianity.

You know why we love the hero's journey pattern so much? We love it because it agrees with our deepest sin and our love for our most beautiful idol: to be our own god. There has been only one hero — and even that hero exists within the enduring mystery of the Trinity. There has been only one hero — and he didn't seek to be his own god. That should be worth more to us than it is.

The hero's journey insists that the pursuit of being our own god will be rewarded by the God we've found a way to accommodate in our idolatry by making him into the one who gets our back when the challenge is too great. We tell the story in a way that assures us he's all about helping us transcend our ordinary world, win the Big Showdown, the BS, and then return as triumphant heroes to the places we once considered quite adequate homes.

We believe in a God who handles the special effects and who would have us be the stars of the show. We love stories like that. We want a God who will make us superhuman, and we don't care much, really, about who he is.

Oh, and here's where the really tasty part comes in. Once God ratifies our status as superhuman, we ascend to a place where "the little people" can no longer understand the mysteries of our greatness. There's nothing more for them to offer us. The Shire has turned foolish and small, and it's ridiculous to think we would submit ourselves to it once again. Those fools in Zionsville could never understand the phenomenal transcendence that comes when a superhuman punk kid gives up selling margarine to watch *Dukes of Hazzard* with retarded guys three days a week. No way — the magic is far too heady for the drones to comprehend. For heroes like we want to be, our only option is to set sail for the faraway magic land of sweet sunsets and rosy syrup. We become gods, and we become free from any accountability — an accountability that would be redundant anyway, since we've become so wise and all that.

We will go through hell itself if we believe that on the far side God will remove the shackles incumbent with our status as contingent beings. As good American Christians we get the added bonus of also having God there to serve us with protection, an ordered universe, and dynamite parking spaces at the mall. That's what a hero is to us, however well we may hide behind coy arguments to the contrary.

Here's what sucks. Frodo Baggins. Luke Skywalker. Me. What do you call someone who leaves the ordinary world on a hero's journey, but fails? What do you say when the Force isn't with you, when the eagles don't show up, or when Melinda dies anyway? There is no such thing as a failed hero. You're either a hero or a failure. Or, as fans of gallant efforts and better luck next time would have it, a fool for believing success was important when it never was. If you die on the way to blow up the Death Star, you fail. If you die on the way to destroy the ring, you fail. If you die on the way to the cross, you fail. And if you fail, you are a failure. And if you are a failure, you don't get to sail away to the land of sweet sunsets and rosy syrup.

That's the problem with the hero's journey. We are all somewhere other than the land of sweet sunsets and rosy syrup. We're all somewhere between the Shire and the pit of fire. We're all somewhere between Tatooine and the Death Star. There's an eagle, but the whole journey's a big, abusive waste of time. The eagle isn't circling, removed and aloof, waiting to pick us up at some location we struggle to reach. The eagle's just as happy to pick us up and take us to the new place from wherever we are.

The only reason it seems like eagles show up at the dramatic climax is that for most of us, it takes a dramatic climax to understand that we're simple hobbits from the Shire with no business tempting such potent enemies.

And the ring? If you ask me, it sounds a lot like the collection on the back of a crab — just a bunch of junk that makes us feel invisible to the bad guys who are only as big a threat to us as we keep them, by our refusal to accept an undeserved rescue from a God who has experienced all of our fear, shame, and sin, and who likes us quite a lot anyway.

This already is the land of sweet sunsets and rosy syrup. The kingdom is among us. We are more than conquerors. This list of worldview-builders goes on and on too. There is a journey for us, and there are trials and challenges, no doubt about that. But what's radically ignored by the world Christians resemble so closely is that our journey begins on the far side of the *Star Wars* credits, or on the page after *The Lord of the Rings* says, "The End."

Success in life is not measured by what we achieve, but by what we come to admit. It is not measured by how far we journey, how many zombies, goblins, or droids we slay, or by our return as champions. It is not measured by how much good I do for any of the people I get paid to care about. Success in life is measured by what we come to admit.

We succeed when we admit we need a ride from an eagle.

We succeed when we admit that we are sinners in the hands of a God who has every right to obliterate us but has instead invited us to journey — to tour — this playground of a planet and this universe of spirit and beauty and joy. We succeed when we admit — as a child admits when she closes her eyes and soaks in her mother's song—that there is nothing for us to do to earn God's love but to receive it.

The point is not the triumph — the point is the deliverance. The point is not the hero — the point is the deliverer.

I want the hero in me to die.

I admit I need my Lord.

Now what?

CHAPTER 38

REALITY = RELATIONSHIP

"I'll tell you now what," Jon the Philosopher says. "Your problem is that you're working from a substance ontology instead of a relational ontology. What you're missing, specifically, is a Trinitarian relational ontology that's rooted in love. So long as you cling to a substance ontology you will be stuck with feeling the limitations it ensures — namely the perpetual creation of idols and dualism."

"Oh, good, Jon. So that's my problem. I'll just go fix that real quick. Can I buy that remedy when I get a refill on my Mountain Dew — use it to complement my burrito?"

Jon shrugs and nods.

"What in the world did you just say to me?" I exclaim.

He takes a deep breath and looks around, his eyes settling on the pressed foam cup from which he's been drinking his Mountain Dew.

"What is this?" he asks.

"It's a cup."

"How do you know?"

"It's a cup."

"No, it is shapes of material glued together to make a different shape. The definition of 'cup' comes from the relationship the cup has with its use and with its user. The question is not whether or not the materials that comprise the cup exist — the question is from whence the definition of that collection of materials derives its value. The collection of shapes is not a cup until we call it so. And that is definition rooted in a relational perspective."

"Uh."

"Tell me who you are, without using your name."

"I'm the friend you've gotten to know over the past however-long."

"Do it again, without using your name or those terms."

"Okay. I'm a guy. A Christian. An American."

"If we kept going, each layer of abstraction would create a new sense of vagueness in you, right?"

"Sure, because we'd be moving more and more to the generic."

"And if we kept going, and going, where would we get to?"

"I guess eventually I'd even have to eliminate my actions or choices, right?"

"Maybe."

"It seems like the smallest answer, the prime number of me, would be something like 'semi-sentient meat puppet.'"

Jon laughs. "That's a good phrase for it. Let me make sure why you picked it. Did you mean because your soul and body are tied together, so you can't be reduced to anything smaller than your whole self, but anything you do or think is more than your basic, meat-puppetish self?"

"Yeah. I didn't have the words for it, but yeah, that's what I meant," I say.

"Good. So we're on the same page. What you just described is the ground floor for substance ontology," Jon says. "It doesn't feel like it orients you properly, does it? It's not adequate to the task of living, and it's less than a full description of you."

"Right. And it seems to me that the image of God that we bear has to be more than just a static attribute. It seems like any fair description of me would have to make room for what I do, what I think, and how I'm known."

"Let's go back to the cup. It's just a collection of shapes until I see its value as a cup." He raises his eyebrows to ask if I'm with him.

"Okay."

"So its value comes from my relationship with it."

"Well, its definition does. I don't know how my interaction with the cup determines its value." I challenge, really not sure where he's going with all of this.

"Okay, let's say we wanted to use this cup to bail out a clogged toilet. Once we did that, would you still call it a cup?"

"I might, but I would sure think of it differently and wouldn't use it as a *drinking* cup again."

"So you may call it a bailing device or something like that to make it clear that you wouldn't want your Mountain Dew served to you in it anymore?"

"Right."

"Okay. So a different use can create a different definition. Right?"

"Sure."

"Which means that definition comes from the relationship between object and mover, right?"

"Yes."

"What about value? Would this object have as much value as a toilet bailing device as it has as a drinking cup?"

"It would depend on whether I needed a drink or wanted to bail out a toilet."

"Exactly. Relationship determines value. Good. Is this object better designed to function as a drinking cup or as a toilet bailing device?"

"Drinking cup."

"Why?" Jon nods a little and makes a subtle gesture toward himself to encourage me to play along.

"Well, there's no handle on it. And there'd be no use for the straw. The plastic lid would have to be removed during the bailing, and then wouldn't be all that helpful afterward because it isn't leak-proof."

"What about the insulating value of the pressed foam?"

"Not so important with clogged toilets."

"But handy with Mountain Dew."

"So I'm a semi-sentient meat puppet whose definition and value come from the relationship I have with Jesus."

"No."

"Why not? Isn't that what we just said?"

"No. We determined that with a substance ontology the ground floor is that you are a semi-sentient meat puppet who is used by God."

"So what am I in a relational ontology?"

"Roll with me for another minute with the cup thing, but ask yourself something real quick — do your personal experiences with Jesus lead you to believe that he sees you as a semi-sentient meat puppet, or as something far more precious?"

"He's quite fond of me."

Jon grins. "That's right, Mr. Ragamuffin. So the disconnect between what you've experienced with Jesus and what you're forced to call yourself with a substance ontology should tell you something's not quite right."

"Yeah. I know. That's why I brought up the whole deal about idols and crab shells in the first place."

"Okay. So with this cup, does it matter what we put into it? Does it have greater value for some things than others? Would it be just as valuable holding hot tea as it is for the sipping of this heavenly nectar we call Mountain Dew?"

"It depends on what I feel like drinking."

"Good."

"But there's no handle to it, and I don't drink hot tea through a straw, so it would not be quite as well-suited for use with tea."

"What about Wite-Out?" Jon asks.

"Why Wite-Out?"

"Wite-Out would eat the cup. So first off, using the cup to hold Wite-Out would change the definition into something other than cup — we'd probably call it a container or something instead. Then it would change the cup's value because the cup is far larger than we'd need for Wite-Out, and it isn't airtight so it would be a lousy storage device. And the Wite-Out would immediately begin to destroy the cup itself, so even its substance value would be ruined. The very existence of the cup, not just its definition or value, would be compromised and eventually eliminated by assigning it the wrong definition and task."

"The wrong relationship can destroy."

"So relationship trumps substance."

"Jon, can we move forward? I brought this up because I hurt and because I feel like I don't know what else to do with work and with my faith. I've spent too much time trapped in metaphors, and I feel like I've been burned trying to force myself into a life that proves them out. I think I'm starting to understand what you're saying, so can we shift away from the cup and back to me and God?" I ask.

"Sure. Try this. How would you feel if you learned you were just a cup, stacked in a column, waiting to be used however the next customer — God — chose to use you?"

"I thought you said I wasn't a meat puppet."

"How would you feel?"

"Not good."

"Why?"

"Because I'd feel invisible."

"Why? You'd still be individual and you'd still have a purpose to your existence."

"I guess because I wouldn't feel at all special or unique. Or loved."

"Okay. What if you were the customer's very favorite cup? Let's say you went everywhere with the customer and were lovingly washed every night and raved about for how great you felt in the customer's hand, or against the customer's lips. Would that help?"

"This is really silly."

"Would it help?"

"Yeah. It would."

"Why?"

"Because I would feel important, and because I would feel loved."

"But dude, you're just a cup. Wouldn't a customer who loved his cup so much sort of creep you out?"

"Hey — you created this weird object lesson."

"And man, what if you wore out and failed the customer? He'd be crushed, and you'd suddenly be useless and discarded."

"Well, I am just a cup, after all. He'd get over it."

274

"Exactly."

"Exactly what, Jon?" I laugh, totally turned around.

"Exactly this. Jesus is not some freak with an obsessive-compulsive love for meat puppets. And our value is not defined by our utility. At some point we all wear out and fail, but Jesus does not say, 'Oops, there goes another meat puppet. That sucks! Oh well, I'll go get me another one tomorrow.'"

"Whoa."

"Yeah. You can be as pretty and as loved as you want to be in a substance ontology, but what you have to make room for is the idea that you will only have your utility to justify you. You can have a place for heaven, but it can really only be about being put out to pasture or else being recycled for new utility elsewhere."

"But what about all of that stuff about relationship defining value?"

"It does. But unlike the relationship you have with a cup, the relationship with God, particularly within the fullness of the Trinity, is all about love — about affection."

"I don't get it."

"You know the 'For God so loved the world' verse. Then you have Jesus saying, 'I will send you the Counselor, who comes from the Father.' But before that Jesus said, 'No one comes to the Father except through me.'"

"Yeah? So?"

"On this side of the sending of the Holy Spirit, it works like this. The Father loves the world through the Spirit, who loves Jesus through us, who love and come to the Father through the Son, who pours his love and mercy out upon the world through the work of the Holy Spirit and the Church."

"Give me a second to draw the lines on that one."

"It comes down to this. We do not love Jesus with our own love. We love him with a love that is poured into us by the Spirit. I don't want to get into the whole deal about free will or what is required for salvation and all of that, so don't let yourself spin off on that, but it seems to me that life within the kingdom of God is a matter of choosing between the creation and the Creator. Between the voice and the Speaker, as you've said before. Between substance thinking and relational thinking. You told me that symbols can never be the things they stand for — so why would you continue to try to relate to the symbols when everything in you points to a living God you only have to admit a preference to know instead? Substance thinking can only lead to despair because it makes your existence as a contingent being a horribly vulnerable thing; but if you allow yourself to let go of that, to look instead to all of the language about God's love and God's desire to interact with us — to have the affectionate relationship define everything — you become a supremely durable being. You become part of the love, and all of the physical realities and tasks set before you are merely the setting for your expression and reception of love. Seriously, what could be better news than that? Why not choose it?"

"How?"

"Dude, it's love. Just let go of the old thinking as you find it. Choose love where you find fear. God's pretty good about showing the way of the kingdom if you can remind yourself, 'Love is what's real.'"

"Okay."

"You know what else relational ontology does?"

"What?"

"It kills the word 'should.' It kills the phrase 'supposed to,' and the preamble, 'a Christian is' whatever. Think about your world and how different it would be if you could get past trying to do it right.

You're a classic first-born child, running scared and trying to stay out of trouble so you can get the praise. Even where you've seen that you need God, you seem to keep trying to impress him again. It doesn't work that way with God. You are a Christian, and what makes you a Christian is not your works. You will do works because you are a follower of Jesus, but as soon as you turn it around and start looking to do things to define your Christianity, to impress God or to enjoy the control, you stop following Jesus and instead head out after marching orders of your own invention. Jesus said that the yoke he would give us was easy and the burden light. He pulls the weight beside you, carrying what you cannot. He protects you. You do not have to fear the attacks that may come, because he will be there. The foolishness of the Gospel is the foolishness of being naked in a world that believes it can protect itself if it covers itself."

Dinner with Jon is like this sometimes.

CHAPTER 39

TEARING

Today is a big day at Bud's. The board has continued to be split for over a year now, and the more timid — meaning fiscally conservative — faction wants to divert needed money away from the Warehouse and into a micro-lending pool, forcing Bud's to downsize and relocate. We've nursed the operation through, but it's hardly thriving. I'm not the right guy to make it work, either. Pastor Ellison and Jeff have said that I've been the right guy for this time, but I know that I'm not going to be able to fix it.

The timid portion of the board also wants to revisit my compensation package, which has included bonuses recently because we've had a couple of big months. The more aggressive board members are willing to play meltdown over the issue of diverting funds, and this is the first meeting where I haven't known exactly how things will go. If the timid side wins, it could be enough to kill the business, and it would be a huge betrayal of support within the larger ministry umbrella. The route I've seen to Bud's continued success would be ruined, and in addition to the insult I'd feel from the lack of support and the shortsightedness of the choice, I'd be placed into the situation where my departure would certainly be a huge disappointment to the people who want to see the business succeed. If the timid side wins, and I leave, the subsequent collapse of the business would be blamed explicitly on me. But if the timid side wins, and I stay, I have absolutely no idea how I can do anything but ride the ship to the bottom of the sea.

If the aggressive side wins, there will be ramifications on the relational front, both within the Bud's board and within the board of our parent ministries, and at least one person would quit his job with the ministry. I don't see how today will be good news, and for as much as I've thought and jockeyed and prayed about today, I have no idea how it came to this, or what real-life things could have been done differently. It seems like this crossroads was set before I was hired.

I'm thinking about this as my white sedan floats through traffic up Broadway, smooth and rising northward like columns of bubbles in a champagne glass, the air-conditioning on for the first time this year. Traffic brakes briefly as a pedestrian in a tie cuts hurriedly across from the west side of the road to the east. He's running to another man, who is trying to resuscitate a homeless woman on the sidewalk. She is quite clearly dead. The soles of her feet are black from city soot, and her pink dress is hiked to just past her hip, her head on the cement. She is wearing no underwear, and there is blood trailing from there to the ground. She looks vaguely familiar. Traffic picks back up, and I move with it, eager to get to the board meeting.

The whole board is present, and tensions run high. Years of frustration spurt out in unproductive ways. Fingers are pointed, blanket statements tossed about. The timid side has prepared for this, and after more than a year of losing these encounters, the die is already cast. They will win, and I will lose. It is not a surprise, and while it would usually be emotionally wrenching, I keep thinking about the woman on the side of the road.

It was Maria, the woman I gave the hundred dollars to so she could get herself and her kids out of the snow. And I drove right past. There was no good place to pull over. I'm wearing a white dress shirt and didn't want to sweat. I had a very important meeting to get to. She was already dead anyway. There was nothing I could have done. But none of that matters because in that moment I looked at her from within my bubble, and she could have been the evening news. She wasn't even real to me.

But she was real. She was a human being lying dead on the sidewalk, just feet from me, and she may as well have been a dog for all I did in response. There was a time when her father bounced his baby girl on his knee. There was a day when she learned to jump rope. Another when she learned to ride a bike. Once she may have sold lemonade for five cents a glass. She didn't deserve to die alone, violently, at the hands of another or under the influence of some drug by which she will be defined in the coroner's report and medics' cold defensive humor.

And where are her kids this morning?

Bad things happened to her along the way, and each was a tragedy. Each was an assault on the little girl who didn't deserve to be scarred. Each was a crime. And no one came to her rescue. No one brought justice for the abuse. The family of man failed her. Maria fell through the cracks because the rest of us live on false scaffolding that prevents us from seeing her, let alone reaching down to save her. Maria died, and I drove by. I had a very important ministry to go fight for. Maria died because I was more important than she was. And so were the ideas and principles and rescue program I serve. I was so busy with myself and my idols and my designs to efficiently do God's work that I could not be interrupted. Not many of us live in ways that leave us open to interruption. We want the protection of organizations. We want to "have people for that." Specialists in following Christ so we won't have to do it ourselves. Maria died, and somewhere someone will use her as evidence that we need more ministries to help people like Maria.

That's not true. What we need is to be willing to stop the stupid car.

CHAPTER 40

TATTERS

I left Bud's the next week, after it became clear that my salary itself was going to push the budget beyond what it could bear. The board chairman said he didn't blame me, that he wouldn't expect his employees to show up if he didn't pay them. Frankly, it was a convenient time to get out of a situation I didn't know how to manage.

I don't know what the timid board members thought because I never spoke to any of them again. I assume they felt betrayed and as though my departure proved things about my lack of commitment, faith, and maturity. The Bud's employees didn't really seem to care. During my time at Bud's, we ran through about twenty employees. We called each of them successes in some way, but the fact is that the only two whom I'd even begin to think of as successes are Marcos and Juan; the others either quit from frustration or were fired for not measuring up. One board member helped Marcos buy a house. Juan left soon after I did, and I'm told he's a highly valued employee at a hotel downtown, which is no surprise because he was a rock at Bud's too.

It tore me up to see that the guys didn't really care that I was leaving, that it was such a matter-of-fact thing. I have to assume they felt the same abuses I discovered we were perpetuating upon them, and saw what an unimpressive person that made me, all sizzle and no steak.

I haven't spoken with Henry or Sam Love, or Hungarian Vince since I left that job. I have no idea what became of Cajun Critter from Turnaround, or of Insane Jarrod who faked speaking in tongues. While Pastor Ellison has become one of my best friends, he has his own church now and I've had no contact with any of the other people from Five Points Christian Church. I see Jeff Johnsen from time to time, and I hear bits and pieces about how things are going for Mile High Ministries. His continued presence and enthusiasm for what he does haunts me, and I have so much respect for him that I assume there's a piece I'm missing, but frankly I'm too worn out to search for it. Bud's has moved to a smaller building owned by one of the board members, and continues on. It turns out that my departure caused the same sort of energy input that greeted me, with people refusing to let it die. It sounds like the board found an outstanding leader, and things are looking good for the business.

I spend time with Skinny Robert, and with Jon, and with David and Danielle and their new son, Cole. I see Rachel now and then, but we're hardly close anymore. We all attend different churches, and none of us seems very happy about them. I had a girlfriend for three months, but she broke up with me when she decided I wasn't ready to commit. I went from that discussion directly to the reggae bar and ended up a good deal less than sober.

It's been a year since Bud's. I wear a tie to my new job with a plumbing distributor, and I have become extremely familiar with the different urinal plumbing options. I've automated some of the processes the distributor uses in soliciting business and in measuring customer satisfaction. I lost some weight on the Atkins diet, and then regained it. Everyone in the office knows I'm a Christian.

I am most certainly not a tremendous man of God. I never was. The world I came to Denver to build blows gently in ashes and tatters.

What I do have is a peace. I think about love being real. I see that I am loved. I see that I love. I see that my love causes me to act, to plan, to partner, to care; but what is rapidly fading is a desire to prove myself or impress anyone. My parents are terrified that I'm depressed and that I'll kill myself because I don't have stories of greatness to lob their way. I'm still weeding my way out of a huge pile of dead symbols, stupid crab camouflage, and personal brand affectations and lies. It turns out my addictions to approval and to food run far deeper — and consume far more love from me — than I ever realized before. It has been hard. It is still hard. But there's this: I'm seen. I am learning to be me, to let God see me, and to understand that I am not the things that stand for me.

It's ash and tatters, but it won't always be. The despair is gone.

CHAPTER 41

SALVAGE

I'm home for another Christmas. Dad and I play a game of chess in his study. He asks about priorities. I tell him my first priority is God, my second is my family, my third is my life's work, and my fourth is my friends.

He asks if I think my life reflects my priorities.

I haven't been truly active in a church for two years, since Robert, Jon, and a couple more of us left Church in the City for reasons I've pretty much forgotten now. I am not doing any ministry work, and it's still hard for me to say that just being a decent guy who points to God now and then is enough. So the God part isn't where I'd like it to be.

I live a thousand miles from my family, who have all ended up staying in Zionsville. Both brothers married high school sweethearts whose families are also from town. I don't talk to my brothers except when I'm home for holidays. I'm not satisfied with the family part.

My life's work? I don't know what it is. It certainly is not selling wax toilet rings. I spend more than fifty hours a week at a job, not a career or a passion. I'm not content with the job item on my priority list.

Friends? Rachel and I seem guaranteed to continue on the same path — unable to be a couple, but still close enough to get in the way of new romances. Skinny Robert has a fiancée he'll be marrying in August, which makes him pretty unavailable. Jon is a recluse with his wife and Doberman. David and I are still good, but our connection isn't enough to build a world around. I'm in Pastor Ellison's Bible study every Friday night, but they have a new baby and he's incredibly busy. There is nothing keeping me in Denver but habit and pride.

My dad makes the point that it may be worth thinking about moving home, where at least I will be around family.

Here's what I'm coming to understand: We all want to be loved, and we all want to be seen, and we all hate being made invisible by the agendas and social regulations of people and structures that don't see us for who we are. We want to express who we are, and to be loved through those definitions, through those arguments to importance, but our own expressions and definitions will always become our prisons — we will pay and pay until we get what we want.

But we cannot know who we are apart from the love of Jesus. We will pay and pay until we get the wrong thing, because we do not know how to build the right thing. I wanted to be loved as a radical follower of Jesus, a learned man devoted to doing good in the name of the Lord.

I don't get to decide how I'm loved. And it takes a dedicated fool to be arrogant about the sorts of love he's willing to receive.

It will take some time to give up insisting which parts of me a person sees, and I am afraid to be loved for areas other than the areas

I think represent my true self. I want to control the decorations of my shell, the chosen symbols and shorthand of my deeper self. I want to be loved and seen for the person I believe myself to be, not for the person others have decided I am. I don't know if a person can ever get that from his family.

But maybe it's time to try. I tell my dad I'll pray about it.

CHAPTER 42

EASTER

Pastor Ellison has a sort of game he plays that I really like. If there's a big decision to make about life, say something like whether or not to move home after five years of trying different ministry stuff, he does what he calls "putting it in the tomb." He prays about it and gives it to God during Lent. If the idea returns to him at Easter, it's alive and he acts upon it. If it doesn't come back, if it dies in the tomb, then nothing comes of it. That's what I did this year.

Easter was fifteen days ago. Rachel and I attended Ellison's thriving multiracial suburban church, where he has absolutely hit his stride. We sat in the front row. She wore a yellow sundress. As we sang the doxology, I wrapped my arm lightly around her waist, and I knew it was time to leave Denver.

Rachel cried when I told her, saying that once I left she would be alone. There's little point in analyzing her, but it would be fair to say that she'd keep me near to her for the comfort no matter what it cost me. And there's little point in analyzing me, but it made me feel good that she was sad about my departure. I don't know if there's a parallel to find between our relationship and the one between the Church and the world, and I'm tired of thinking about it.

My other close friends understood and encouraged me, though they said they would miss me. I've run out of time to tell quite a few other people, who will find out weeks and months from now that I've left town.

I gave notice the next day and have been offered an interview at the plumbing distributor's Indianapolis branch, which I'll probably look into until I figure out something else to do.

My mom says there's a girl in Zionsville named Christine who she really wants me to meet.

My stuff is packed and ready to go. It took a Ryder truck, packed to the ceiling, to get me here. I'm returning home with all my stuff fitting into my white sedan and part of an SUV.

My father's SUV arrives, driven by my two brothers. My sister-in-law is in the back seat. After five years of misunderstanding, mocking, and condemnation — all of these things going both directions — in the end, when everything else has fallen apart, it is my brothers who have driven twenty hours to take me home. I am overcome by the moment. Maybe I didn't know what was important until right now. It is not family — it is the love and relationship that exists beneath the family connection. We share a portion of our identity. My brothers look like me, fair and stocky, strong and loyal, nice guys who are well aware of their flaws, but who are willing to love anyone willing to be loved. I am proud to be one of them.

We load my things into the SUV and pull away from my place an hour later. They don't even want to spend the night; they would rather push to make the round trip all at once. We do stop by the Coors brewery for a tour and samples, and lunch beneath the mountains in Golden, and then we hit the road.

They don't understand me. They have no idea what I'm talking about with most of the ideas I spray around. They have no interest in the version of myself I've sought to create. They have no desire to offer the prophet respect in his hometown. All they care about is that their brother is coming home.

What a relief.

ACKNOWLEDGMENTS

This book would not exist if my wife, Christine, had not carried the load for us — relationally and financially — while it took me two years to learn that life's truly valuable dreams are worth pursuing wisely, instead of the all-or-nothing approach I fell into. The title, *My Beautiful Idol*, still carries wounds of irony about the sacrifices I stole from her, even if the lessons we learned along the way have made us stronger and happier today. She jokes with friends that this book will be a success when she can buy it at Costco, or when she sees me on the *Daily Show with Jon Stewart* (which somehow beat out *Oprah*). Christine is my perfect partner, and I love her with all my heart.

I didn't have the patience or the humility to follow traditional channels when I first finished the manuscript, and if it were not for Chris Anderson's blog about The Long Tail, I would never have chosen to self-publish and work the system as I have. This is an exciting time in the world of technology and art, and while there are still a great many economic and structural details to sort out, it's great news for people whose primary passion is to share their story.

Ultimately I believe all we can really offer one another are our prayers and our testimonies; this is an era where both can be amplified, and for that I'm grateful.

My agent, Kathryn Helmers, found me because I'd paid to associate my self-published work with *Blue Like Jazz* at Amazon. She also represents Donald Miller, and the fact that she was checking on her other client's success, followed the cross-reference, and then saw enough in what I'd done to get in touch with me about selling the manuscript to a real publisher was an amazing first impression for me. Every impression since has only strengthened my opinion of the woman and the agency services she provides.

Angela Scheff, Becky Shingledecker, and the rest of the editorial team at Zondervan — and John Topliff, who has repeatedly stepped up from the marketing side of things — are better people than I am. They work with patience and humility — and keen eyes and ears — that lovingly respect both the voice of the author and the sensibilities of the Christian bookselling world. Far from compromise, what they really do is create a safe, honoring common ground where important things can be said, and can be said in ways that continue to earn the author the privilege of being heard by the audience he loves.

Along the way, there have been countless words of encouragement from people who kept me believing this wasn't a complete waste of time.

Their names and faces stream in front of me now, and there are simply too many to list here. You and I both know who you are. Thank you, thank you, thank you.

I value your thoughts about what you've just read.
Please share them with me. You'll find contact information
in the back of this book.

Share Your Thoughts

With the Author: Your comments will be forwarded to
the author when you send them to *zauthor@zondervan.com*.

With Zondervan: Submit your review of this book
by writing to *zreview@zondervan.com*.

Free Online Resources at
www.zondervan.com/hello

 Zondervan AuthorTracker: Be notified whenever your
favorite authors publish new books, go on tour, or post
an update about what's happening in their lives.

 Daily Bible Verses and Devotions: Enrich your life
with daily Bible verses or devotions that help you start
every morning focused on God.

 Free Email Publications: Sign up for newsletters on
fiction, Christian living, church ministry, parenting, and
more.

 Zondervan Bible Search: Find and compare
Bible passages in a variety of translations at
www.zondervanbiblesearch.com.

 Other Benefits: Register yourself to receive online
benefits like coupons and special offers, or to participate
in research.